allergy–free cooking

allergy-free cooking

OVER 50 ENTICING AND TASTY
RECIPES THAT AVOID KNOWN FOOD
PROBLEMS

CONSULTANT EDITOR:
MAGGIE PANNELL

LORENZ BOOKS

This edition published in 2001 by Lorenz Books

© Anness Publishing Limited 1999, 2001

Lorenz Books is an imprint of Anness Publishing Limited
Hermes House, 88–89 Blackfriars Road, London SE1 8HA

www.lorenzbooks.com

This edition distributed in Canada by Raincoast Books, 9050 Shaughnessy Street,
Vancouver, British Columbia V6P 6E5

A CIP catalogue record for this book is available from the British Library.

Publisher: Joanna Lorenz
Executive Editor: Linda Fraser
Designer: Carole Perks
Reader: Marion Wilson
Production Controller: Don Campaniello
Photographers: Karl Adamson, Nicki Dowey, Michelle Garrett, Amanda Heywood
and William Lingwood (Pictures on pp9 and 12 Tony Stone Images)
Recipes: Angela Boggiano, Jacqueline Clarke, Carole Clements, Joanna Farrow, Christine France,
Shirley Gill, Christine Ingram, Kathy Mann, Lesley Mackley, Maggie Mayhew, Sallie Morris, Jennie
Shapter, Kate Whiteman, Elizabeth Wolf-Cohen and Jeni Wright

1 3 5 7 9 10 8 6 4 2

NOTES

For all recipes, quantities are given in both metric and imperial measures and,
where appropriate, measures are also given in standard cups and spoons.
Follow one set, but not a mixture, because they are not interchangeable.

Standard spoon and cup measures are level.
1 tsp = 5ml, 1 tbsp = 15ml. 1 cup = 250ml/8fl oz

Australian standard tablespoons are 20ml. Australian readers should use 3 tsp
in place of 1 tbsp for measuring small quantities of cornflour, salt, etc.

Soy Sauce contains wheat flour and is unsuitable for wheat or gluten-free
diets. As a substitute, use Tamari which is also made from soya beans but
which is rice based. It is readily available from health food shops.

Many commercial stock cubes contain MSG, which can be made from wheat
starch, and are therefore unsuitable for wheat- or gluten-free diets. Look for
stocks or bouillion cubes/powders that are labelled gluten-free or fresh, or
chilled stocks, which are available from larger supermarkets, if there is no
time to make homemade stock. Always read the ingredients list on any food
product to check that it is "safe" to eat for any special diet.

Medium eggs are used unless otherwise stated.

ALLERGY-FREE RECIPES
The recipes in this book have an at-a-glance guide to the foods
that each is free from:

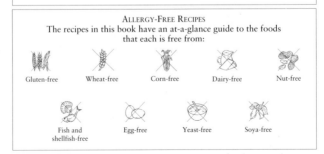

| Gluten-free | Wheat-free | Corn-free | Dairy-free | Nut-free |

| Fish and shellfish-free | Egg-free | Yeast-free | Soya-free |

CONTENTS

INTRODUCTION

If you've ever developed a bad migraine or an irritating skin rash, or perhaps a digestive problem or a stuffy nose that doesn't then become a cold, it may be that the condition was caused not by illness but by something to which you are allergic or sensitive. Depending on the severity of the symptoms, this may be either a mild, short-term nuisance or a more serious condition, such as asthma or coeliac disease. It's not known just how common "allergies" are. Potential causes are numerous and can be difficult to identify.

The aim of this chapter is to help you discover if something that you're eating or drinking could be the cause of your symptoms. Once you've tracked down the cause of the problem, this book has helpful advice on how to adapt your diet to be nutritionally balanced while excluding anything to which you're sensitive. By investigating your symptoms and excluding suspect foods from your diet, you can discover the culprit(s) causing the reaction and use these delicious and easily prepared recipes to help you enjoy a healthy, allergy-free life.

WHAT IS AN ALLERGY?

An allergy is a reaction that occurs when the body's immune (defence) system overreacts to a normally harmless substance, causing irritation, disability and sometimes even fatality. A substance that causes an allergy is called an allergen and can be anything in the environment – whether it's something ingested, inhaled or that touches the skin – that causes an adverse reaction. Among the most commonly found allergens are pollen, house-dust mites, pet hair, insect stings, chemicals or food or drink.

Our immune system usually protects us from harmful foreign invaders, such as viruses and bacteria, that might otherwise cause illness. In the allergic person, however, the system believes that the allergen is damaging and reacts to it accordingly. A special type of antibody, called IgE (immunoglobulin E), is produced to fend off the threatening substance, triggering the release of chemicals, such as histamine. These cause the unpleasant symptoms, such as rashes, inflammation or wheezing, that are often associated with an allergic reaction.

HOW COMMON ARE ALLERGIES?

It is not known just how common allergies are as the potential causes are numerous and can be difficult to identify. It is not even known exactly how many people react badly to certain substances since many cases are mild enough to be undetected or may be misdiagnosed: an individual's desire to label a condition can lead them to a mistaken conclusion about a cause and its effect.

It has been suggested that as many as 25 per cent of the population will suffer from an intolerance at some point in their lives. Asthma, eczema and hay fever, for example, are very common and appear to be on the increase. This may be a consequence of a number of factors, including increased air pollution, greater use of chemicals, modern living conditions and more stressful lifestyles.

Surprisingly, the onset of an allergy or intolerance can occur at any age and the substance may be something that has previously been tolerated. Equally, sensitivity can be outgrown, and troublesome symptoms completely disappear.

THE DIFFERENCE BETWEEN ALLERGY, INTOLERANCE AND SENSITIVITY

Strictly speaking, the word allergy should only be used to describe a specific response caused by an over-reaction of the immune system. An intolerance, however, is a broader term describing any unpleasant reaction to an offending substance. Hyper-sensitivity can be used as a general description

Above: Chocolate and drinks, such as tea, coffee and cola, contain caffeine.

Above: A migraine can be caused by eating chocolate or cheese, or by drinking red wine.

covering both allergy and intolerance, although none of these should be confused with food aversion, which has psychological roots.

There are many different causes of food intolerance, which may be linked to the behaviour of various enzymes or bacteria in the body. Lactose (milk sugar) intolerance, for example, is not an allergic reaction but occurs because a person has insufficient lactase enzyme, which is needed for the digestion of lactose.

There are also a number of substances in food that can cause a reaction in some people. Caffeine in tea, coffee, chocolate and cola, for instance, can bring on palpitations and restless behaviour, while amines found in red wine, chocolate and cheese can trigger a migraine. These are not true allergic reactions, although the term allergy is frequently loosely used for describing all sorts of food intolerance.

Right: Pet hair may cause an allergic reaction that results in irritation to the eyes, nose and skin, and difficulty in breathing.

NON-FOOD ALLERGENS

Discover the cause of your allergy, then take action to avoid the substance or to minimize your exposure to it. Could one of these allergens be to blame?

House-dust mites – Modern homes often have fitted carpets, double glazing, central heating and poor ventilation, providing ideal conditions for house mites to thrive. You should vacuum regularly, wet wipe surfaces, consider wood and lino flooring rather than carpets, and blinds rather than curtains. Open windows as often as possible.

Insect (bee and wasp) stings – These may cause pain and swelling and occasionally anaphylactic shock.

Jewellery – Metal allergy (especially to nickel) can cause skin irritation.

Medicines – Aspirin and penicillin and other antibiotics can cause an allergic rash. Aspirin may cause asthma.

Pets – Fur and feathers may be responsible for allergic rhinitis, asthma and eczema.

Pollen – Hay fever is a common allergy. It causes itchy eyes, sneezing and a blocked nose, especially when the sufferer ventures outdoors, and particularly in early summer. To reduce the symptoms, it is best to avoid over-exposure by closing windows and wearing sunglasses.

Toiletries and cosmetics – Perfumed products can be a problem so try changing to a pure formulation or using non-allergenic make-up.

Above: Beauty preparations and soaps with non-allergenic formulae are now widely available and popular for their purity.

The Healthy Diet

Before investigating whether your symptoms could be caused by an allergy or intolerance to any particular food, it is important first of all to establish that you are eating healthily. A poor diet could be the reason for certain conditions, which may disappear once your diet is improved. So let's take a closer look at what constitutes a healthy diet. We all know that variety and balance are important, but how do you put that theory into practice? Healthy eating is one of the most important ways in which we can look after our health. It doesn't mean banning foods on the grounds that they're high in fat, sugar or salt. It means choosing a wide variety of foods to obtain the balance of nutrients that are needed for the development and maintenance of a healthy body.

How to Choose a Healthy Balance

Bread, cereals and potatoes – These are the starchy carbohydrate foods that provide sustained energy as well as important vitamins and minerals and some protein. Wholegrain types, such as wholemeal bread and brown rice, and potatoes in their jackets, are a particularly good source of dietary fibre, which reduces the risk of intestinal disorders. This group of foods also includes pasta, white rice, breakfast cereals, oats, couscous, polenta, beans, lentils and starchy vegetables, such as yams and plantains. Carbohydrates should form the main part of your meals. They are not fattening or high in calories provided you don't add much fat or sugar when cooking or serving them.

Above: Bread and vegetables, such as plantains and potatoes, are rich in carbohydrate.

Fruits and vegetables – These foods are packed with valuable minerals and the antioxidant vitamins, beta carotene (a form of vitamin A) and vitamins C and E. Antioxidant vitamins are believed to help protect the body against free radicals, which can lead to degenerative diseases, such as heart disease and some cancers. Fruits and vegetables are also low in fat and calories and contain a type of fibre that may help to reduce blood cholesterol. With such a wide choice available, eating the recommended "five a day" is easy and produce doesn't always have to be fresh. Frozen, dried and canned fruits and vegetables may be more convenient and help to add variety.

Dairy foods – This group of foods, which includes milk, cheese and yogurt, helps provide protein and B group vitamins and is an excellent source of calcium, which is needed for strong bones and normal blood clotting. However, dairy foods can be high in saturated fat so only eat moderate amounts. Choose skimmed

How to Boost your Fruit and Vegetable Intake

- Slice fruit, such as banana or peach, on to your breakfast cereal.
- Keep the fruit bowl well stocked to provide healthy snacks.
- Stock up with packets of dried fruits, such as apricots and prunes, for popping into lunch boxes.

- Top jacket potatoes with chilli beans, ratatouille or sweetcorn to make a satisfying lunch.
- Serve raw vegetable crudités with a dip for a starter.
- Stir-fry vegetables with rice or noodles to make a quick meal.

- Pack sandwiches generously with crisp salad ingredients.
- Boost soups, stews, casseroles, home-made burgers and pasta sauces with extra vegetables.
- Make fresh fruit salads and dried fruit compotes for quick desserts.

Above: Chicken and meat are major sources of protein, but choose lean, skinless cuts.

Above: The protein and fatty acids found in oily fish are essential to a healthy diet.

or semi-skimmed milk and other low-fat dairy foods, which provide just as much calcium as full-fat varieties.

Meat, fish and other protein foods – These are major sources of vitamins and minerals in our diet (red meat especially provides iron and Vitamin B_{12}), but they don't need to be eaten in large amounts. Choose lean meat, poultry and game and opt for healthy, low-fat cooking methods, such as grilling, steaming and stir-frying. It is a good idea to eat fish at least twice

a week, especially oily varieties, such as herring, sardines, mackerel, salmon and tuna, because they contain Omega-3 fatty acids, which are thought to help reduce the risk of heart disease. Other foods in this group, such as pulses (peas, beans and lentils), nuts, eggs, quorn and soya products, provide alternative protein sources for vegetarians and people on special diets.

Occasional foods – Biscuits, cakes, crisps, chips, pies, pastries, puddings, ice cream, chocolate, sweets, fats, salad

THE ADVANTAGES OF A HEALTHY WHOLE FOOD DIET

- Your weight will take care of itself without having to diet or count calories.
- There's less chance of developing degenerative diseases, such as heart disease, some cancers, bowel disorders and osteoporosis.
- You will have more energy and feel and look more vibrant.
- Tooth decay and gum disease will be less of a problem.

dressings and soft drinks all tend to be high in fat and/or sugar (and therefore high in calories) and they are less nourishing than other foods. These foods should be eaten in moderation; too much of them can lead to weight gain and dental problems, especially if they are eaten between meals or as substitutes for healthier choices. Alcohol, too, should be drunk in moderation. It is a rich source of calories and provides energy, but it has very little nutrient value.

ORGANIC FOODS

These are foods that have been produced without the use of chemical pesticides and fertilizers, or genetically modified materials. The strict rules governing all products sold as organic are guaranteed by certification bodies.

Organic foods cost more to produce and are therefore more expensive than other foods, but growing public demand has led to much greater availability, which should in time make their price more competitive. The range of organic foods now available includes a variety of fresh produce as well as meat, dairy and cereal foods, preserves, chocolate, wines and beers.

Left: Besides fresh fruit and vegetables, organic produce includes wine and beer as well as bread and cheese.

CEREAL FOODS

Because people are more likely to experience sensitivity to foods that they eat frequently, those who are sensitive to cereals make up one of the most common food intolerance groups. There are two different cereal-related allergies that can arise. The first is an extreme intolerance to gluten (the protein found in wheat, rye, barley and oats), which causes coeliac disease, a condition that is medically well recognized and affects between 1 in 1,000–1,500 people. The second is an intolerance to a single cereal, such as wheat (most common in Western countries), corn (most common in North America where corn products are widely eaten), and rice (although this is rare). People who have intolerance to one cereal can usually eat other cereals without any adverse affects.

COELIAC DISEASE

Coeliac (pronounced see-lee-ack) disease is caused when the protein complex gluten irritates and damages the lining of the small intestine. The consequence is that food is poorly absorbed and causes malnutrition.

Gluten protein is found in wheat and is similar to the proteins that are found in rye, barley and oats, which means that all these cereals have to be avoided. Sometimes oats may be tolerated as they contain less gluten.

The condition may first become apparent in a small child, when weaning foods are first introduced, but it is more common for the disease to be diagnosed in adulthood. The cause is unknown but the condition is inherited and can therefore run in families.

Once coeliac disease has been diagnosed, it is necessary to follow a gluten-free diet for life. Unlike some other food intolerances, people cannot outgrow this condition but, by avoiding gluten, can enjoy a full and healthy life.

THE SYMPTOMS OF COELIAC DISEASE

Typically, the symptoms of coeliac disease include:
- diarrhoea
- vomiting
- weight loss
- anaemia
- extreme tiredness
- recurrent mouth ulcers

An infant with coeliac disease will fail to grow and thrive when cereals that contain gluten are introduced to its diet. He or she will be miserable and lethargic with a poor appetite, pass pale, bulky and offensive soft stools, and develop a pot belly. It is important that the condition is diagnosed early in order to prevent severe malnourishment and poor health, so seek medical advice if you are concerned.

WHEAT ALLERGY

If you have an intolerance or allergy to wheat or other cereals, the symptoms may be less serious than for coeliac disease but can still cause discomfort. Many of these symptoms may have another cause so it is impossible to draw immediate conclusions.

You may suffer, for example, from any or all of the following:
- persistent digestive upsets
- fatigue
- joint pain
- asthma
- rhinitis
- skin complaints

FOOD LABELLING

The words "gluten-free" appear on products purported to be suitable for people with a gluten intolerance. However, it is worth checking the ingredients list for less obvious gluten sources: binder; cereal protein; corn starch; edible starch; food starch; modified starch; rusk; thickener or vegetable protein.

DIAGNOSIS

Because the symptoms of coeliac disease are both apparent and specific, it is likely to be quickly diagnosed. Your doctor may suspect the condition if you are suffering from its typical symptoms and he or she will probably refer you to a hospital outpatients' department for an intestinal biopsy, which is performed under mild sedation. This will confirm whether or not the condition is present. Once coeliac disease has been diagnosed, you can adjust your diet to dispel the symptoms. However, sufferers from coeliac disease are more likely to also intolerant of other foods, such as lactose and soya, so further investigation may be necessary.

If you are suffering from a wheat or other cereal intolerance, with vaguer and more general symptoms, it may take longer to identify the cause of your problem. The culprit(s) can usually only be accurately discovered by following an exclusion and challenge diet.

OTHER CONDITIONS RELATED TO GLUTEN INTOLERANCE

Those suffering from the rare skin disorder *dermatitis herpetiformis* can be helped by following a gluten-free diet. There are several other conditions that may be alleviated, but more medical research is needed to support this theory. These conditions include:
- multiple sclerosis
- rheumatoid arthritis
- Crohn's disease

Above: Some common foods containing wheat include bread, cake, pasta, wheat cereals, biscuits and processed soups.

Above: Barley, rye and oats can be eaten by people with a wheat intolerance but not by those with a gluten intolerance.

Above: Foods that should be avoided if you have an intolerance to corn include cornflakes, corn oil, tortillas and popcorn.

WHAT FOODS DO YOU NEED TO AVOID?

Gluten intolerance – Unfortunately wheat and cereals make up a large part of the diet, so if coeliac disease is diagnosed, it means making considerable changes. As well as cutting out wheat-based foods, such as bread, flour, pasta, semolina, couscous, bulgur and certain breakfast cereals, wheat is also used in processed foods, such as cakes, biscuits, crispbreads, pastries, puddings, soups, sauces, gravy, stuffing mixes and sausages. You will also need to avoid rye and barley (including malted bedtime drinks) and possibly oats, depending on the nature of your intolerance. However, never start a gluten-free diet without first consulting your doctor.

Wheat intolerance – If only wheat is suspected, you will need to exclude all sources of wheat, wheat starch and wheat protein (gluten) from your diet. However, you will still be able to enjoy other cereals, such as barley, rye and oats. This type of intolerance may not be a lifelong condition. Sometimes small amounts of wheat can gradually be reintroduced without causing further problems.

Corn (maize) intolerance – Corn does not contain any gluten. However, it can still cause problems, especially if it is eaten frequently. Avoid cornflakes and other corn cereals, polenta, corn oil, tortilla, corn snacks, sweetcorn, popcorn, cornflour and custard powder. Check the ingredient labels on manufactured foods for cornflour, corn (maize) starch, cornmeal and corn oil.

ALTERNATIVE CEREAL FOODS

A restricted diet can seem rather daunting initially, especially if it means giving up a lot of the foods that have previously been enjoyed. However, there are plenty of alternative products available from supermarkets, health food shops and specialist companies.

Changing to a gluten-free diet takes adjustment but your meals can still be

Above: Gluten-free alternatives to wheat include chick-peas, rice, buckwheat, polenta, soya, potato flour and tapioca.

interesting and nutritionally balanced. Specially produced gluten-free flour, as well as potato flour, arrowroot, cornflour, buckwheat flour, soya flour, ground rice or chick-pea flour (besan) are all good substitutes for wheat flour. Cooked and puréed starchy vegetables can often be used for thickening soups and sauces.

There is a wide range of commercially made gluten-free foods, such as breads, cakes, biscuits, pasta, muesli, crispbreads and rusks, some of which may be available on prescription. Gluten-free products may include wheat starch so be aware if you are sensitive to wheat rather than gluten. It is advisable to check ingredient labels on manufactured foods.

ENSURING A HEALTHY DIET

You can enjoy all meat, fish and poultry other than products prepared in batter, breadcrumbs or sauce. Eat plenty of fresh produce and a variety of other cereal products to ensure that your diet isn't lacking in nutrients and dietary fibre. Dairy products and eggs provide a good source of nourishment as long as there isn't a further intolerance evident. A dietician will be able to offer valuable advice in making dietary changes and maintaining a good nutritional balance.

MILK AND OTHER DAIRY PRODUCTS

Milk and dairy products play an important part in our diet but can cause an adverse reaction in some people. Depending on the nature of the sensitivity, this may only be a temporary condition and some people may be able to tolerate some dairy products. Luckily, there are many alternative milks and dairy-free products available to ensure that people with a dairy intolerance can still enjoy a balanced and varied diet. Always seek medical advice before making any drastic dietary changes as dairy products make a valuable nutritional contribution and shouldn't be excluded without good reason.

WHAT IS LACTOSE INTOLERANCE?

This relatively common condition affects mostly adolescents and adults, and some children. It is more prevalent among Eastern Europeans and people of Asian or African origin, where milk has traditionally played a less important part in the diet after weaning. An intolerance occurs because insufficient lactase enzyme is produced to digest properly the lactose sugar present in milk, so it passes undigested into the large intestine, causing bloating, diarrhoea and excessive wind.

Lactose intolerance may also occur temporarily following a bout of gastro-enteritis, especially in young children, or as a consequence of gastric surgery or chemotherapy, all of which can destroy lactase production.

Whether you are suffering from a mild or severe, permanent or temporary intolerance, a low-lactose or lactose-free diet is advised, although just how strict it has to be varies between individuals. You may find you can tolerate small amounts of regular milk without ill effect, especially if it is included within a meal, or that you can eat hard cheeses, such as Cheddar, which are low in lactose. Yogurt may be acceptable, too, as the bacteria in yogurt help to digest lactose.

If you or your doctor suspect a lactose intolerance, there are tests that can confirm it. This may involve testing the stools for acidity, which is what usually happens in the case of infants, or measuring blood sugar and breath hydrogen after eating a standard amount of lactose.

ARE YOU ALLERGIC TO MILK?

The number of people who are allergic to cow's milk is unknown but if you suffer from asthma, eczema or rhinitis, dairy products may be the problem.

An elimination and challenge diet procedure is likely to be your best approach for discovering a milk allergy.

FOODS TO AVOID

Dairy products include all types of cow's milk and its derivatives, cream, butter, cheese, quark, yogurt, fromage frais, crème fraîche, skimmed milk powder, casein (also caseinates and hydrolyzed casein), whey syrup sweetener, hydrolyzed whey protein, whey sugar, non-fat milk solids, lactalbumin and lactose.

If you are following an exclusion diet, you will also need to avoid dishes made using milk. Although you can still enjoy foods such as milk puddings, custard sauces, pancakes, batter, quiches

Hard cheeses, such as Cheddar, Red Leicester and Parmesan (left), contain less lactose than soft cheeses and may be eaten by some people who are lactose intolerant, as may yogurt (below), which contains bacteria that help to digest lactose.

Above: Many cakes, custard, savoury pies and quiches contain dairy products, as do some store-bought sauces.

and flans by replacing cow's milk with an alternative "safe" milk. Milk and dairy products are also often hidden ingredients in manufactured foods, such as cakes, biscuits, ice cream, chocolate, most margarines and spreads, puddings, dessert mixes, soups and dips.

All the major supermarkets will provide detailed lists of milk-free products on request. Look out for items labelled "dairy-free" or "suitable for vegans".

KEEPING A HEALTHY NUTRITIONAL BALANCE

Milk and dairy products are usually the main source of calcium in the diet and provide valuable amounts of protein, some B vitamins (particularly B_2/riboflavin) and vitamin A. There are plenty of other foods that can provide calcium and it is important, if you are excluding dairy products either for the short or longer term, that you regularly include a variety of these in your diet. It is vital to maintain an adequate supply of calcium in order to build strong teeth and bones and to help prevent osteoporosis (brittle bone disease) in later life. Check with your doctor or a dietician that your dietary intake is adequate. If it is not, they may recommend that you take a calcium supplement.

Above: Broccoli, leafy greens, sardines, pilchards, apricots and figs are all good non-dairy sources of calcium.

NON-DAIRY CALCIUM SOURCES

- broccoli and dark green, leafy vegetables
- nuts (especially almonds)
- dried fruits
- seeds
- canned sardines or pilchards (you need to eat the soft edible bones)
- bread
- pulses
- soya beans
- tofu (bean curd)
- calcium-fortified soya drinks and cheeses

ALTERNATIVE MILKS

You may need to try several before finding one that suits you, as these too can cause a reaction. Goat's and sheep's milk contain less lactose than cow's milk but are not lactose-free. Other alternative milks include oat drinks, rice drinks and coconut milk.

Goat's milk – This has a slightly tangy taste. Yogurts and a wide range of cheeses are also available.

Sheep's milk – This milk is thicker and creamier than cow's milk because it has a higher fat content. It tastes slightly sweet and is ideal for making milk puddings.

Soya drinks – Available fresh and in long-life cartons, soya drinks are lactose-free, usually low in fat and can be sweetened, unsweetened and flavoured. They are often fortified with calcium and vitamins.

Lactose-reduced milk – This long-life, full-cream product is made from cow's milk and has had most of the lactose removed.

WATCHPOINT

Alternative milks are not suitable as a main drink for infants under 12 months old. A dietician can advise about specially modified milks that are suitable for the allergic child.

OTHER PROBLEM FOODS

Any food has the potential to cause an allergic reaction or intolerance in susceptible individuals, but certain foods are known to be common allergens.

If you suffer from any of the symptoms associated with food sensitivity, such as rashes, wheezing, abdominal discomfort or migraine, start by investigating the typical suspect foods. If the reaction is immediate, you may be able to identify the culprit fairly easily but if there is a delayed reaction, then this is obviously much more difficult.

Sometimes foods that you particularly like – and therefore eat in large quantities – can be responsible for causing reactions. It could be that you have a sensitivity to the very food you crave.

If you think that a food sensitivity may be the cause of certain symptoms or illness, don't immediately leap to conclusions and start restricting your diet. A detailed investigation is usually necessary before an accurate diagnosis and recommendation can be made, under the supervision of your doctor, dietician, or a consultant allergy specialist.

NUTS
Peanuts are a common culprit, as are other nuts, such as walnuts, brazil nuts, hazelnuts and almonds. In cases of extreme allergy, they can trigger "anaphylaxis", which is potentially fatal. Sesame seed allergy, although not as common, can be just as severe. Not all reactions are as violent as anaphylaxis and milder responses, such as vomiting, urticaria, itchy tongue, coughing and wheezing, can be treated with a fast-acting antihistamine available from chemists.

Nut or sesame allergy is generally a lifelong condition and those with a peanut allergy are likely to have other allergies and suffer from asthma, eczema and/or hay fever.

Nuts are a popular food and are widely used in cakes, biscuits, confectionery, marzipan, breakfast cereals, salads and vegetarian foods as well as nut oils (some refined oils are safe) and peanut butter. Many ethnic dishes, such as satay sauce, contain nuts and they're also used in a wide variety of manufactured foods, so you need to check the ingredient labels carefully. Sometimes manufacturers use the warning "may contain nut traces" to cover themselves, but companies are being urged to tighten up production controls and to use accurate labelling.

Foods containing sesame seeds include hummus, tahini, halva, burger buns and sesame oil, and they are also widely used in the baking industry.

Above: Many kinds of nuts are associated with food sensitivity but peanuts can cause a severe – sometimes fatal – reaction.

FISH AND SHELLFISH
Healthy eating advice encourages us to enjoy more fish, not only because it is low in saturated fat but because the oily varieties are rich in Omega-3 fatty acids, which are believed to help reduce the risk of heart disease.

However, fish and shellfish can cause an allergic reaction in some people. Fish and shellfish sensitivity are two quite separate problems, so you may find one group of fish are tolerated but not others. Likely symptoms include sickness, diarrhoea, abdominal cramps, wheezing, rhinitis, urticaria and dramatic swelling. Simply handling fish, or even just the smell of fish cooking, can trigger symptoms in a sensitive person.

ANAPHYLACTIC SHOCK

This is a the most serious allergic reaction and is life-threatening. It can be caused by fish, sesame seeds, eggs, milk, soya and wheat, wasp or bee stings and some medicines, such as aspirin and penicillin, but the most common is peanut allergy.

Symptoms include facial swelling, shortness of breath, dizziness and loss of consciousness, so it is essential that sufferers are aware of their condition and take every precaution to avoid the offending substance. If you know that you are severely allergic, you should always carry emergency adrenaline treatment. Always inform schools, relatives, friends and anyone who may prepare food for you of your condition. In restaurants, always check with the chef if you are unsure of the ingredients in a dish and, to be on the safe side, order plainly cooked foods. It is also a good idea to wear a pendant or a MedicAlert identification bracelet, stating your food sensitivity, in case there is an emergency. Asthmatics are particularly at risk.

Above: A sensitivity to shellfish is not uncommon and the crustacean group, which includes crabs, lobsters and prawns, is a frequent culprit.

EGGS

This allergy often co-exists with cow's milk allergy (and sometimes with an allergy to chicken) and is therefore relatively common in young children. However, like cow's milk allergy, the sensitivity frequently disappears by the age of two or three. The protein in the egg white is usually to blame, and allergic symptoms may include urticaria, stomach upsets, wheezing and rhinitis. Egg sensitivity may trigger or worsen eczema and asthma, especially in children.

Foods to be avoided include many cakes, biscuits, custard, mayonnaise, salad cream, hollandaise and Béarnaise sauces, meringues, soufflés, lemon curd, egg noodles, batter mixtures, pancakes, and also some sweets and chocolate products. In some recipes the egg or eggs may be simply omitted.

Above: Fresh and dried pasta and noodles, mayonnaise and lemon curd contain eggs.

Check the ingredient labels on manufactured foods for egg white or egg yolk, albumen, egg protein, dried egg and egg lecithin. Quorn, which is a meat alternative made from a mushroom plant, also contains egg and should therefore be avoided.

YEAST

Yeast sensitivity is sometimes blamed for a wide range of complaints, such as fatigue, thrush, stomach bloating, headaches, itchy anus and even PMS (pre-menstrual syndrome). A yeast-free and sugar-free diet is often recommended for this condition, in which case it's necessary to avoid foods containing any form of yeast, mould or fungi, including mushrooms, grapes and mould-ripened cheeses. Bread, pizza, yeasted pastries, yeast extract, beer, wine and cider, dried fruits, vinegar and pickled foods, cheese and fermented dairy products, malted milk drinks, tofu and soy sauce will all be off the menu and you'll need to check labels for hydrolyzed protein and leavening. As yeasts feed on sugar, this needs to be avoided, too.

Soda bread (which uses baking powder or soda as a raising agent), pitta, chapattis, matzos, rice cakes and rye crispbreads provide delicious alternatives to bread. Eating plenty of garlic may help as it's thought to combat an over-proliferation of yeast in the gut.

Above: Mushrooms, grapes and mould-ripened cheeses can trigger yeast reactions.

SOYA

An intolerance to soya bean products is relatively common and may occur if there's already a sensitivity to cow's milk. Other members of the bean family, including beansprouts and peanuts, may also cause a reaction. To follow a totally soya-free diet, check food labels carefully for tofu, lecithin (E322), soya oil, soy sauce, soya beans, textured or hydrolyzed vegetable protein (TVP). Vegetable oil sources should always be checked as soya oil is often included in blended oils and many vegetarian and gluten-free products may contain soya.

OTHER POSSIBLE CULPRITS

Cheese, chocolate, coffee and citrus fruits (often referred to as the Four Cs) are classic migraine triggers. Alcohol, too, can cause a problem, especially red wine, sherry and port. These foods contain vasoactive amines, which dilate the blood vessels, provoking migraine in susceptible people. Try avoiding these trigger foods and see if the migraines stop, although if you've been a heavy coffee drinker, you may, to begin with, experience headaches caused by caffeine withdrawal. Simple changes to your diet can also help prevent recurrent headaches so be sure to eat regular meals (low blood sugar can precipitate headaches) and drink plenty of water to prevent dehydration.

Strawberries commonly cause urticaria due to the release of histamine soon after eating the fruit. The itchy rash will probably disappear a few hours later.

Citrus fruits (especially oranges) are known to aggravate eczema so avoid these if you have this skin condition.

WHAT ABOUT ADDITIVES?

Additives, especially artificial ones, are often blamed for being the cause of all manner of allergic reactions and may produce behavioural problems, especially in young children, though this is a highly contentious subject. Additives are certainly thought to be responsible for upsetting a minority of susceptible people, but the number affected may well be considerably less than is sometimes suggested.

Additives may be natural (extracted directly from natural products), nature identical (made to match something found in nature) or artificial, but those that are man-made are no more likely to cause adverse reactions than natural additives or, indeed, natural foods. It is important, too, to remember why additives are used in food manufacture. Some are purely cosmetic and are used in response to consumer expectations of colour, flavour and texture, but most fulfil important and necessary functions. Without additives, food would not keep as well, so we would have to shop more frequently. There would be a greater risk of food poisoning and we would not be able to enjoy the wide range of convenience foods that we've grown to expect.

WHY ARE ADDITIVES USED?

Additives perform a number of different functions, and they are categorized and grouped according to their function, usually by E number. The E number indicates that the additive has been approved safe by EC regulations. Those listed are the main categories but there are many others, including anti-caking agents, acidity regulators, and so on.

Colours (E100s) – These are used to restore colour lost in processing (e.g. canned peas) and to make food look more appetizing. Many are natural colourings, coming from foods such as red peppers, grape skins and beetroot.

Preservatives (E200s) – These help keep food safe for longer by preventing the growth of micro-organisms which would cause decay, spoilage and food poisoning. These additives protect our health, reduce wastage and allow us to eat a wider choice of foods all year round.

Antioxidants (E300s) – Used to protect fats and oils in food from turning rancid, changing colour and deteriorating through oxidation. Vitamin E (E306) is used as a natural antioxidant in vegetable oil and ascorbic acid. In fruit drinks vitamin C (E300) prevents the fruit turning brown.

Emulsifiers and stabilizers (E400s) – Emulsifiers help blend ingredients, such as oil and water, together and stabilizers prevent them separating again (as in soft margarines and salad dressings). Thickeners and gelling agents add smoothness to the texture.

Flavourings – A complex range of natural flavourings and artificial chemicals are added to various foods. As yet they do not have any serial numbers.

Flavour enhancers – These help bring out the flavour of foods, the most common is MSG (monosodium glutamate/E621). Wherever possible, manufacturers prefer to use stocks, herbs and spices for boosting flavour.

Artificial sweeteners – These are used more and more frequently in place of sugar because they are lower in calories and better for dental health. Saccharin, aspartame and acesulfame-k are the principal artificial intense sweeteners used.

WHICH ADDITIVES MAY BE A PROBLEM?

Preservatives – Some asthmatics are sensitive to sulphites (E220–E227), such as sulphur dioxide. Sulphite preservatives are used in beer, wine and cider but, as yet, alcoholic drinks are exempt from ingredient labelling laws. Sodium benzoate (E211), another preservative used in soft drinks, sweets, jam and margarine, can cause problems for asthma or urticaria sufferers and has been linked with hyperactivity in children.

Artificial colours – These are recognized as upsetting sensitive people, so many manufacturers, acting in response to consumer demand, have reformulated their products to remove them. The azo dyes, which include tartrazine (E102), a yellow colour used in soft drinks and crumb coatings, may be particularly troublesome. Tartrazine has been linked with hyperactivity in children and also affects asthmatics. Annatto (E160b), which is a natural colour, may also trigger asthma attacks and rashes.

Flavour enhancers – MSG is a widely used flavour enhancer, particularly in Chinese dishes. Some people develop allergic reactions, including headaches, nausea, dizziness and palpitations, on

Above: Alcoholic drinks, such as beer, wine and cider, contain sulphite preservatives but are not subject to ingredient labelling laws.

Above: The flavour enhancer monosodium glutamate (MSG) is often added to Chinese restaurant food.

eating MSG. These reactions have been given the popular name of "Chinese restaurant syndrome". You may want to check with take-aways and restaurants whether MSG is used and ask for it to be omitted.

Hyperactivity in Children

Most children are naturally bounding with energy and can sometimes behave badly. This is all part of growing up and learning social boundaries. It shouldn't be confused with hyperactive behaviour, which can be aggressive, unruly and out of control, and makes it virtually impossible for the child to concentrate or settle for long and intolerable for the rest of the family. In some cases, artificial colours and preservatives may be implicated but take advice from a dietician before jumping to conclusions.

Avoiding Additives

Most supermarkets produce lists of "additive-free" foods. Flashes on packaging stating "no artificial preservatives, colours or flavouring" may also be helpful. Check the labels carefully (all additives must be listed by category and E number or name), and avoid any that you believe cause a reaction. Wherever possible, choose fresh foods.

Could You Be Suffering From an Allergy?

The first step in finding out whether you have an allergy is to make an appointment with your doctor to discuss your symptoms and rule out other illnesses. True allergies, which usually provoke an immediate and acute reaction, are generally straightforward to diagnose (so the offending food can be avoided), but in most cases of food intolerance, identification can be very much more difficult. (Testing for gluten or lactose intolerance has been discussed under cereals and milk and dairy products.)

Detection and Testing Methods Used

There are no quick tests for detecting food intolerances. It is hoped that on-going research projects will provide treatments for allergic conditions and that a greater understanding of the causes will enable better prevention.

The skin prick test and the radio-allergosorbent test (RAST) are the most common tests although even these may give false results.

An elimination and challenge procedure is the best way of discovering which foods are causing a problem, but severe exclusion diets shouldn't be followed long term as they may undermine the nutritional status of the allergy sufferer.

The Skin Prick Test

In this test, a liquid containing an amount of the suspect allergen is placed on the skin. The skin is then pricked to allow the substance to seep under the surface. If the person undergoing the test is allergic to the substance, histamine is released from the sensitive reactive cells and the skin shows an itchy, red weal.

This test can be useful for identifying environmental allergies, such as pollen or cat hair sensitivity, but is not reliable for food allergy testing or for detecting food intolerances, where the immune system is not involved and where the reaction is often masked or delayed. However, extreme allergic disorders, such as anaphylaxis, do usually give a positive skin prick test.

The RAST Test (Radio-allergosorbent Test)

This test measures IgE antibodies in the blood that allergic people make in reaction to specific substances. It may be helpful for detecting true allergies but not food intolerances.

Elimination Diets

These diets are the most accurate means of discovering a food intolerance. Suspect foods are eliminated from the person's diet to see if the symptoms subside, then the foods are reintroduced to see if the symptoms return.

Even if you have some idea about which food(s) are causing problems, you should not attempt an exclusion diet on your own, or you may create nutritional deficiencies. Your doctor may refer you to a special hospital unit or a clinic for further investigation or arrange for you to see a dietician if dietary changes are to be considered.

Desensitizing Methods

Some private clinics claim to be able to cure patients of their allergies using a course of injections of a dilute solution of the allergen. As yet, however, these desensitizing methods are not widely recognized by the medical profession.

TESTING FOR FOOD ALLERGY

Diet investigation is often used to try and discover the cause of food sensitivities. Depending on which food(s) are suspected, the diet may be relatively simple or involve the dieter in a substantial amount of thought and commitment.

In cases of multiple food intolerance, it is far more difficult to discover the whole problem and, because psychological factors may influence a person's perception of how a food affects them, blind testing may be advised so that an accurate diagnosis can be obtained.

Food intolerances are often not lifelong sensitivities. People find that after a rest period the offending food can be reintroduced gradually. However, the food should only be eaten infrequently; eating too much or too often may trigger a repeat of the previous symptoms.

Different clinics and specialists will vary in their approach towards dietary testing, so follow the advice given by your own dietician. Whatever the diet, it is essential that you stick to it rigidly as any lapses will affect the validity of your results.

SIMPLE EXCLUSION DIETS

If you have a fairly good idea about which single food is causing you a problem, it is a simple matter to exclude it from your diet and see if the symptoms disappear or improve. It is quite easy to avoid some foods, such as cheese, red wine and citrus fruits, but if a major food group, such as dairy products or wheat is suspected, you will need to take professional advice from a dietician on how to modify your diet safely without missing out on important nutrients. After avoiding the suspect food for a few weeks, try

Below: Common trigger foods, which cause food intolerances and allergies, include dairy products, such as milk and yogurt, wheat, nuts, citrus fruits and drinks, coffee, chocolate, eggs and shellfish.

eating it again and see if the symptoms return. If you have experienced a severe allergic reaction to a particular food, such as peanuts, don't attempt to try the food again. You already know the cause of the problem and are strongly advised not to risk repeating the reaction.

ELIMINATION DIET TIPS AND GUIDELINES

● Don't choose a busy time, whether at work or at home, to undertake an elimination diet; you need to be stress-free.
● Prepare and plan ahead, so that you don't run out of suitable foods and can easily cater for other members of the family.
● Do not skip meals.
● Try to base your diet on fresh foods as much as possible.
● Stick to plain cooked dishes because using a lot of ingredients in recipes will make detection all the more difficult.
● Avoid eating out, or if you do, choose plainly cooked dishes.
● Make a note of the ingredients used in any manufactured foods.
● Plan some non-food treats for yourself, such as a trip to the hairdresser, a manicure or a sauna, so that you don't focus all your attention on your diet.

MULTIPLE FOOD EXCLUSION DIET

If it's suspected that there is a dietary cause for your symptoms but the offending food is not known, it may be suggested that you cut out common trigger foods, which are known to cause problems most frequently. These foods include milk and dairy products, eggs, shellfish, wheat, citrus fruits, nuts, coffee, chocolate and azo dyes and also possibly corn, yeast and soya.

You will need to follow this diet for two to three weeks to see if any improvement occurs. If symptoms ease or disappear, the excluded foods should

Below: A strict elimination diet permits only foods, such as lamb, turkey, rice, potatoes, broccoli, cauliflower and pears, that rarely cause allergy problems.

then be reintroduced individually, allowing an interval of several days between each. If the symptoms reappear, you have your answer – although several repeat exercises may be necessary to be sure of the diagnosis.

If there is no improvement while following the diet, either some other food could be responsible (and you may be advised to try the more restrictive "few foods" diet) or you will need to investigate other, non-dietary causes.

STRICT ELIMINATION DIET

This very strict diet consists of only a few basic foods that are rarely known to cause a reaction. Because it severely limits the food selection, a strict elimination diet is only advised in extreme cases where medication does not provide any relief. Foods that are commonly allowed include lamb or turkey, potatoes, rice, pears, cauliflower or broccoli (and sometimes other vegetables), sunflower or olive oil and bottled water. The exact range of permitted foods may vary at the discretion of your consultant.

The diet is followed strictly for two to three weeks, then foods are reintroduced one by one, and any change of symptoms observed.

RARE FOODS DIET

This is basically the same as the strict elimination diet, except that some more unusual foods, such as exotic fruits and unusual vegetables and meats, are allowed. The theory behind this diet is that people are less likely to react to foods that they have not eaten (or rarely eaten) before. If symptoms still persist on this diet, then the likely diagnosis is that the person is not food-sensitive and that some other factor is responsible, or that the person has an undiagnosed medical condition.

FASTING

This is a drastic measure that is not generally advised because of the risk of severe nutritional disorders that may

---

FOOD DIARY

Date : *Monday 24th*

Meal	Food / Drink	Time taken	Symptoms
Breakfast	*orange juice* *2 slices of toast* *spread with butter* *& marmalade* *cup of tea*	*7.45am*	
Mid-morning	*cup of coffee* *chocolate biscuit*	*10.30am*	
Lunch	*cheese sandwich* *packet of crisps* *strawberry yogurt*	*12.30pm*	*Migraine about* *2.00pm*
Mid-afternoon	*cup of tea* *jam doughnut*	*3.00pm*	
Evening meal	*grilled fish* *new potatoes and peas* *glass of white wine*	*7.00pm*	

Additional Notes
Difficult day at work – felt very stressed and tired.
Might be starting a cold, sneezing a lot and felt rather blocked up.

---

affect the balance of your health. It is not advisable to attempt such an extreme regime, whether for intolerance testing, weight loss or any other dietary reason.

KEEPING A FOOD DIARY

Keeping a food diary is useful, both as an initial exercise to find out which foods you eat and whether you are following a healthy, balanced diet, and also when you are following an exclusion or elimination diet.

The food diary can help you discover if you really do have a true food intolerance or sensitivity, or whether your symptoms may have other, non food-related causes. Stress, tiredness and even the menstrual cycle can all aggravate a condition. Write down everything that you eat and drink, any symptoms that appear, and when or if they worsen.

A detailed food diary will also be a helpful aid for your doctor or dietician when they are trying to reach a diagnosis and may help them see where to make any dietary adjustments. Remember that symptoms may not appear immediately after eating an offending food. Any reaction may happen hours – or even days – later. You can't presume that the culprit is something you ate at your last meal. In addition, a sensitivity reaction to food may be worse one day than another. All this makes the detection process quite difficult so you will need to be both vigilant and patient.

ALLERGY-FREE EATING

If you have a food sensitivity and need to follow a restricted diet, it does not mean that your food has to be boring. With the fantastic choice of multi-cultural foods, exotic fresh fruits and vegetables and an increasing range of organic produce available from supermarkets and health food shops, there will always be plenty of alternative foods to replace those that you may need to avoid.

EATING OUT

A food sensitivity does not mean that you can't eat out any more, but you will have to think ahead, do a little planning and inform anyone who will be cooking for you and needs to know about any problem foods.

Exactly how careful you need to be will depend on the nature of your sensitivity and the severity of the reaction. Some foods, such as fish, oranges, tomatoes or strawberries are easy to avoid, while others, such as wheat or dairy products will be more difficult because they are common ingredients used in a wide variety of dishes. If you suffer from a severe allergy, such as peanut anaphylaxis, it is absolutely essential that you avoid the offending food.

DINING INVITATIONS

If you have been invited to a friend's home for a meal, it is polite and considerate to warn your host if there's something you are unable to eat. If you are vegetarian, for example, you would inform your host beforehand to avoid any embarrassment and the same applies to food intolerances.

If you feel that this creates any difficulty for your host, then offer to contribute a dish, such as a dessert, towards the meal to make catering easier. If you should be served something that you know will disagree with you, don't worry about refusing it, simply explain tactfully exactly why you are unable to eat the offending food.

RESTAURANT MEALS

Be selective about where you eat and choose restaurants that freshly prepare the food. In restaurants where the dishes are bought in ready-prepared,

Above: When you are dining out, choose simply cooked foods so that you can see exactly what you are eating.

the chef or kitchen staff may not have detailed knowledge of the ingredients used in the food.

It may sometimes be advisable to ask to see the menu in advance, then discuss any special dietary requests with the chef. Don't wait until the restaurant is busy or expect a waiter

Below: Eggs are widely used for thickening and enriching sauces and desserts, binding minced meats and glazing pastries.

to have an in-depth knowledge of how dishes have been prepared.

Campaigns about the dangers of severe food allergies have alerted caterers to be aware of the ingredients they use – particularly nuts, seeds and shellfish – and to be helpful should a customer ask about the ingredients in a dish. If there should be any doubts or the chef isn't available, don't guess and trust to luck or try to pick out offending ingredients. Choose a dish that you can rely on to be safe.

WHAT TO CHOOSE

Composite dishes and sauces that contain lots of ingredients are probably best avoided. If you're in a hurry, and haven't time to ask questions, the best option is to choose something simple: plain cooked foods, such as grilled, baked or roasted fish, meat or poultry accompanied by fresh vegetables or a salad, followed by fresh fruit.

SOME DISHES TO AVOID

● Foods that may contain either nuts or seeds, such as marzipan, cakes, breads, biscuits and cheesecakes, hummus, pesto sauce, salad dressings, satay sauce and many vegetarian dishes.
● Indian and Chinese dishes, such as tandoori and tikka dishes, pilau rice, spare ribs, and sweet and sour pork, which may contain artificial colours.
● Asian foods, which may contain sesame oil.
● Stews, sauces and soups, which may be thickened with wheat flour.
● Foods, such as sausages, fish fingers and chicken nuggets, which may contain breadcrumbs.
● Foods that contain "hidden" eggs used for binding, thickening, coating, setting, enriching or glazing.

COOKING FOR CHILDREN

Children are notorious for being picky about food, but it's important not to confuse fussy eating with food allergies and intolerances, which actually trigger a very real physical reaction. Inheritance seems to be a factor in predisposing a child to suffering from allergies. This tendency, where a family may suffer from various allergies, is known as atopy. Although children often outgrow childhood allergies, such as asthma and eczema, those with a family history of allergic illness are more likely to develop other allergic conditions and possibly food intolerance problems.

COMMON ALLERGIES

Milk allergy can start in early infancy when a formula milk or cow's milk is introduced during weaning. The most common symptoms are asthma, eczema, urticaria, allergic rhinitis, vomiting and diarrhoea. Breastfeeding may help to prevent the condition, especially where there is a family history of allergic illness. Lactose intolerance may also occur temporarily following a bout of gastroenteritis in young children. On recovery from illness, and after excluding lactose for a while, the condition usually clears up but always take advice from your doctor or health visitor. Most children outgrow any sensitivity to cow's milk by the age of three years.

Wheat and eggs are also common foods to which children may have a sensitivity, generally showing as asthma or eczema. To reduce the risk of allergies, these foods should not be introduced too early into an infant's diet. It is recommended that wheat and egg yolk are not introduced before six months, egg white not until nine months, and regular cow's milk ideally not before one year. Rice is considered to be the least "allergenic" cereal and is recommended as a weaning food from the age of four months. Look out for the gluten-free symbol on manufactured baby foods and don't be tempted to introduce solids into your baby's diet too early.

If a child does develop an allergy while weaning, always seek professional advice and never attempt an elimination diet without expert guidance. Most children outgrow such problems by the age of five.

Above: Young children can often be persuaded to try adult food if the family sits down together and makes the mealtime into a social occasion.

HEALTHY EATING

A child's diet should be well balanced nutritionally, and meet all his or her requirements for energy, growth, repair and maintenance. The foods don't have to be exclusively healthy – "junk" foods can be very appealing to a child and need not be banned, provided they are not eaten in place of healthier fresh food alternatives and are not the cause of any allergic condition.

If your child does have any food sensitivities, try not to make a fuss about any special diets. Make meals fun and enjoyable, and help your child develop a healthy interest in food by encouraging him or her to help with the shopping and meal preparation.

SCHOOL LUNCHES

If you prepare packed lunches for your child, and some foods are not allowed, make sure your child understands why he or she should not swap items with friends. If the child is to eat a cooked school meal at lunchtime, talk to the school caterers, who are generally happy to discuss and provide for special needs. Although most school catering services no longer use nuts or seeds, you should always inform the school of any severe allergies.

ARE ADDITIVES TO BLAME?

If you think that additives (particularly colourings and preservatives) are causing an allergic reaction or making your child behave badly, then the best policy is to feed the child simple, fresh foods and to cook your own home-made dishes.

Soups, Starters
and Salads

Whatever the season or the occasion, you will find a recipe here to

enhance your meal. There's a range of delicious nutritious snacks,

light lunches and elegant starters to tempt you. Lentil Soup with

Tomatoes or Spicy Potato Wedges with Chilli Dip will warm you on

a winter day. Chilled Summer Tomato Soup or Parma Ham with

Mango will bring Mediterranean flavours to your table in midsummer.

Lentil Soup with Tomatoes

A classic rustic Italian soup flavoured with rosemary.

INGREDIENTS

Serves 4

225g/8oz/1 cup dried green or
   brown lentils
45ml/3 tbsp extra virgin olive oil
3 rindless streaky bacon rashers, cut
   into small dice
1 onion, finely chopped
2 celery sticks, finely chopped
2 carrots, finely diced
2 rosemary sprigs, finely chopped
2 bay leaves
400g/14oz can chopped plum tomatoes
1.75 litres/3 pints/7½ cups
   vegetable stock
salt and ground black pepper
bay leaves and rosemary sprigs,
   to garnish

1 Place the lentils in a bowl and cover with cold water. Leave to soak for 2 hours. Rinse and drain well.

2 Heat the oil in a large saucepan. Add the bacon and cook for about 3 minutes, then stir in the onion and cook for 5 minutes until softened. Stir in the celery, carrots, rosemary, bay leaves and lentils. Toss over the heat for 1 minute until thoroughly coated in the oil.

3 Tip in the tomatoes and stock and bring to the boil. Lower the heat, half cover the pan, and simmer for about 1 hour, or until the lentils are perfectly tender.

4 Remove the bay leaves, add salt and pepper to taste and serve with a garnish of fresh bay leaves and rosemary sprigs.

NUTRITION NOTES	
Per portion:	
Energy	357kcals/1501kJ
Protein	19.6g
Fat	16.6g
Saturated fat	3.9g
Carbohydrate	34.7g
Sugar	6.63g
Fibre (NSP)	6.8g
Calcium	80mg

Spinach and Rice Soup

Use very fresh, young spinach leaves to prepare this light and clean-tasting soup.

INGREDIENTS

Serves 4

675g/1½ lb fresh spinach, washed
45ml/3 tbsp extra virgin olive oil
1 small onion, finely chopped
2 garlic cloves, finely chopped
1 small fresh red chilli, seeded and
   finely chopped
115g/4oz/generous 1 cup risotto rice
1.2 litres/2 pints/5 cups vegetable stock
salt and ground black pepper
60ml/4 tbsp freshly grated Parmesan
   cheese, to serve

1 Place the spinach in a large pan with just the water that clings to its leaves after washing. Add a large pinch of salt. Heat gently until the spinach has wilted, then remove from the heat and drain, reserving any liquid.

2 Either chop the spinach finely using a large knife or place in a food processor and process to a fairly coarse purée.

3 Heat the oil in a large saucepan and cook the onion, garlic and chilli for 4–5 minutes until softened. Stir in the rice, then pour in the stock and the reserved spinach liquid. Bring to the boil, then simmer for 10 minutes. Add the spinach and season to taste. Cook for 5–7 minutes more, until the rice is tender. Serve with Parmesan cheese.

NUTRITION NOTES	
Per portion:	
Energy	292kcals/1215kJ
Protein	12.6g
Fat	14.8g
Saturated fat	4.4g
Carbohydrate	29.5g
Sugar	3.16g
Fibre (NSP)	3.8g
Calcium	470mg

Summer Tomato Soup

FREE FROM

The success of this soup depends on having ripe, full-flavoured tomatoes, so make it when the tomato season is at its peak. It is equally delicious served cold.

INGREDIENTS

Serves 4
15ml/1 tbsp olive oil
1 large onion, chopped
1 carrot, chopped
1kg/2¼lb ripe tomatoes, cored
    and quartered
2 garlic cloves, chopped
5 thyme sprigs, or 1.5ml/¼ tsp
    dried thyme
4 or 5 marjoram sprigs, or 1.5ml/¼ tsp
    dried marjoram
1 bay leaf
45ml/3 tbsp sheep's or goat's milk
    yogurt, plus a little extra to garnish
salt and ground black pepper
marjoram sprigs, to garnish

1 Heat the olive oil in a large, preferably stainless steel, saucepan or flameproof casserole.

2 Add the onion and carrot and cook for 3–4 minutes, until just softened, stirring occasionally.

VARIATION

To serve the soup cold, omit the yogurt and leave to cool, then chill.

3 Add the tomatoes, garlic and herbs. Reduce the heat and simmer, covered, for 30 minutes.

4 Pass the soup through a food mill or press through a sieve into the pan. Stir in the yogurt and season. Reheat gently and serve in warmed soup bowls, garnished with a spoonful of yogurt and a sprig of marjoram.

NUTRITION NOTES

Per portion:	
Energy	84kcals/335kJ
Protein	2.4g
Fat	4g
Saturated fat	0.9g
Carbohydrate	10.2g
Sugar	9.8g
Fibre (NSP)	3g
Calcium	39mg

Pumpkin Soup

FREE FROM

INGREDIENTS

Serves 6–8
25g/1oz/2 tbsp pure vegetable
    margarine
1 large onion, chopped
2 shallots, chopped
2 medium potatoes, peeled and cubed
900g/2lb/6 cups cubed pumpkin
2 litres/3⅓ pints/8 cups chicken or
    vegetable stock
2.5ml/½ tsp ground cumin
pinch of freshly grated nutmeg
salt and ground black pepper
fresh parsley or chives, to garnish

1 Melt the margarine in a large flameproof casserole or saucepan. Add the onion and shallots and cook for 4–5 minutes until just softened.

2 Add the potatoes, pumpkin, stock, cumin and grated nutmeg, and season with a little salt and black pepper. Reduce the heat to low and simmer, covered, for about 1 hour, stirring occasionally, until the vegetables are thoroughly cooked.

NUTRITION NOTES

Per portion:	
Energy	95–71kcals/400–300kJ
Protein	3.2–2.4g
Fat	4.6–3.5g
Saturated fat	1.9–1.5g
Carbohydrate	10.9–8.7g
Sugar	3.9–2.9g
Fibre (NSP)	2.1–1.6g
Calcium	55–41mg

3 With a slotted spoon, transfer the cooked vegetables to a food processor and process until smooth, adding a little of the cooking liquid if needed. Stir the purée into the cooking liquid remaining in the pan until well mixed. Adjust the seasoning and reheat gently. Garnish the soup with the fresh herbs.

Melon and Grapefruit Cocktail

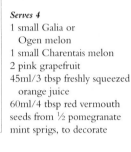

This pretty, colourful starter can be made in minutes, so it is perfect for when you don't have much time to cook, but want something really special to eat.

INGREDIENTS

Serves 4
1 small Galia or
    Ogen melon
1 small Charentais melon
2 pink grapefruit
45ml/3 tbsp freshly squeezed
    orange juice
60ml/4 tbsp red vermouth
seeds from ½ pomegranate
mint sprigs, to decorate

— COOK'S TIP —

If citrus fruits are a problem, substitute alternative fruits, such as kiwi fruits, and use apple juice in place of the orange.

1 Halve the melons and scoop out the seeds. Cut into wedges, peel, then cut into large bite-size pieces.

— NUTRITION NOTES —

Per portion:	
Energy	52kcals/220kJ
Protein	0.8g
Fat	0.2g
Saturated fat	0g
Carbohydrate	9.4g
Sugar	9.4g
Fibre (NSP)	1.1g
Calcium	24mg

2 Using a small sharp knife, cut the peel and pith from the grapefruit. Holding the fruit over a bowl to catch the juice, cut between the grapefruit membranes to release the segments. Pour off all the juice into a bowl.

3 Stir the orange juice and vermouth into the reserved grapefruit juice.

4 Arrange the melon pieces and grapefruit segments haphazardly on four individual serving plates. Spoon the dressing over, then scatter with the pomegranate seeds. Decorate with mint sprigs and serve at once.

Parma Ham with Mango

Other fresh, colourful fruits, such as figs, papaya or melon, would go equally well with the ham in this light, elegant starter. Be sure to buy the true prosciutto from Parma for the best flavour. This dish is amazingly simple to prepare and can be made in advance – ideal if you are serving a complicated main course.

INGREDIENTS

Serves 4
16 slices Parma ham
1 ripe mango
ground black pepper
flat leaf parsley sprigs, to garnish

1 Separate the Parma ham slices and arrange four slices on each of four individual plates, crumpling the ham slightly to give a decorative effect.

2 Cut the mango into three thick slices around the stone, then slice the flesh and discard the stone. Neatly cut away the skin from each slice.

3 Arrange the mango slices in among the Parma ham slices. Grind some black pepper over the top and serve garnished with flat leaf parsley sprigs.

— NUTRITION NOTES —

Per portion:	
Energy	73kcals/275kJ
Protein	6.6g
Fat	2.75g
Saturated fat	1.4g
Carbohydrate	4.7g
Sugar	4.6g
Fibre (NSP)	0.8g
Calcium	7mg

Spicy Potato Wedges with Chilli Dip

Perfect as a starter or light meal, these dry-roasted potato wedges have a crisp, spicy crust, which makes them irresistible, especially when served with a chilli dip.

INGREDIENTS

Serves 2

2 baking potatoes, about 225g/
  8oz each
30ml/2 tbsp olive oil
2 garlic cloves, crushed
5ml/1 tsp ground allspice
5ml/1 tsp ground coriander
15ml/1 tbsp paprika
sea salt and ground black pepper

For the dip

15ml/1 tbsp olive oil
1 small onion, finely chopped
1 garlic clove, crushed
200g/7oz can chopped tomatoes
1 fresh red chilli, seeded and
  finely chopped
15ml/1 tbsp lemon juice
15ml/1 tbsp chopped fresh coriander,
  plus extra to garnish

1 Preheat the oven to 200°C/400°F/ Gas 6. Cut the potatoes in half, then into eight wedges.

2 Place the wedges in a saucepan of cold water. Bring to the boil, then lower the heat and simmer gently for 10 minutes or until softened slightly. Drain and pat dry on kitchen paper.

COOK'S TIP

To save time, parboil the potatoes and toss them with the spices in advance, but make sure that the potato wedges are perfectly dry and completely covered in the mixture.

3 Mix together the oil, garlic, allspice, coriander and paprika in a roasting tin. Add salt and pepper to taste. Add the potatoes to the pan and shake to coat them thoroughly.

4 Roast the potato wedges for about 20 minutes, turning them occasionally, until they are browned, crisp and fully cooked.

5 Meanwhile, make the chilli dip. Heat the oil in a saucepan, add the onion and garlic and cook for 5–10 minutes until soft. Add the canned tomatoes, with their juice, then stir in the chilli and lemon juice.

6 Cook gently for 10 minutes until the mixture has reduced and thickened. Stir in the fresh coriander and serve hot, with the potato wedges. Garnish the potato wedges with fresh coriander and sprinkle with salt.

--- NUTRITION NOTES ---

Per portion:

Energy	344kcals/1439kJ
Protein	6.1g
Fat	17g
Saturated fat	2.3g
Carbohydrate	44.1g
Sugar	5.8g
Fibre (NSP)	40g
Calcium	31mg

Globe Artichokes, Green Beans and Garlic Dressing

Similar to French aïoli, but egg-free and exceptionally garlicky, this creamy, lemon-flavoured dressing makes a perfect partner to freshly cooked vegetables.

INGREDIENTS

Serves 4–6
225g/8oz green beans
3 small globe artichokes
15ml/1 tbsp olive oil
pared rind of 1 lemon
coarse salt for sprinkling
lemon wedges, to serve

For the garlic dressing
6 large garlic cloves, sliced
10ml/2 tsp lemon juice
250ml/8fl oz/1 cup olive oil
salt and ground black pepper

1 To make the garlic dressing, put the garlic and lemon juice in a blender or mini food processor. With the machine switched on, gradually pour in the olive oil until the mixture is thickened and smooth. Alternatively, crush the garlic to a paste with the lemon juice and gradually beat in the oil using a hand whisk. Season with salt and pepper to taste.

2 To make the salad, cook the beans in boiling water for 1–2 minutes until slightly softened. Drain.

3 Trim the artichoke stalks close to the base. Cook the artichokes in a large pan of salted water for about 30 minutes, or until you can easily pull away a leaf from the base. Drain well.

— COOK'S TIP —

Mediterranean baby artichokes are sometimes available and are perfect for this kind of salad as, unlike the larger ones, they can be eaten whole. Cook them until just tender, then cut in half to serve. Canned artichoke hearts, thoroughly drained and sliced, could also be substituted.

4 Using a sharp knife, halve the artichokes lengthways and ease out the choke using a teaspoon.

5 Arrange the artichokes and beans on serving plates and drizzle with the oil. Scatter with the lemon rind and season with coarse salt and a little pepper. Spoon the dressing into the artichoke hearts and serve warm with lemon wedges. To eat artichokes, pull the leaves from the base one at a time and use to scoop a little of the sauce. It is only the fleshy end of each leaf that is eaten as well as the base or "heart" of the artichoke.

FREE FROM

— NUTRITION NOTES —

Per portion:
Energy	416–282kcals/1747–1165kJ
Protein	3.4–2.2g
Fat	44.4–29.6g
Saturated fat	6.4–4.2g
Carbohydrate	4.1–2.7g
Sugar	2.4–1.6g
Fibre (NSP)	1.2–0.8g
Calcium	54–36mg

Olives with Spicy Marinades

INGREDIENTS

Serves 6–8
225g/8oz/1⅓ cups green or tan olives
  for each marinade

For the spicy herb marinade
45ml/3 tbsp chopped fresh coriander
45ml/3 tbsp chopped fresh flat
  leaf parsley
1 garlic clove, finely chopped
good pinch of cayenne pepper
good pinch of ground cumin
30–45ml/2–3 tbsp olive oil
30–45ml/2–3 tbsp lemon juice

For the ginger and chilli marinade
60ml/4 tbsp chopped fresh coriander
60ml/4 tbsp chopped fresh flat
  leaf parsley
1 garlic clove, finely chopped
5ml/1 tsp grated fresh root ginger
1 red chilli, seeded and finely sliced
¼ preserved lemon, cut into thin
  strips (optional)

1 Squash the olives, hard enough to break the flesh, but taking care not to crack the stone. Place in a bowl of cold water and leave overnight to remove the excess brine.

2 Drain thoroughly and divide the olives between two jars.

3 Blend the ingredients for the spicy herb marinade and pour into one of the jars of olives, adding more oil and lemon juice to cover, if necessary. Seal the jar.

4 To make the ginger and chilli marinade, mix together the coriander, parsley, garlic, ginger, chilli and preserved lemon, if using. Add to the remaining jar of olives and seal.

5 Store the olives in the fridge for at least one week before use, shaking the jars occasionally.

—— NUTRITION NOTES ——

Per portion:
Energy	88–66kcals/363–272kJ
Protein	0.4–0.3g
Fat	9.6–7.2g
Saturated fat	1.4–1.1g
Carbohydrate	0.12–0.1g
Sugar	0.12–0.1g
Fibre (NSP)	0.5–0.35g
Calcium	23–17mg

Broad Bean Dip

This dish is similar to hummus, but uses broad beans instead of chick-peas. It is usually eaten by scooping up the purée with bread, but raw vegetable crudités or potato crisps could be served for dipping.

INGREDIENTS

Serves 6–8
115g/4oz dried broad beans, soaked
2 garlic cloves, peeled
5ml/1 tsp cumin seeds
about 60ml/4 tbsp olive oil
salt
mint sprigs, to garnish
extra cumin seeds, cayenne pepper and
  vegetables crudités to serve

1 Put the dried broad beans in a pan with the whole garlic cloves and cumin seeds and add enough water just to cover. Bring to the boil, then reduce the heat and simmer until the beans are tender. Drain, cool and then slip off the outer skin of each bean.

2 Purée the beans in a food processor or blender, adding sufficient olive oil and water to give a smooth soft dip. Season to taste with plenty of salt. Garnish with sprigs of mint and serve with extra cumin seeds, cayenne pepper and vegetables crudités.

—— NUTRITION NOTES ——

Per portion:
Energy	171–114kcals/715–476kJ
Protein	7.5–5g
Fat	11.8–7.9g
Saturated fat	1.7–1.1g
Carbohydrate	9.3–6.2g
Sugar	1.6–1.1g
Fibre (NSP)	7.9–5.3g
Calcium	28.7–19.1mg

Spanish Rice Salad

This rice salad is packed with the flavours of the Mediterranean and would make a good accompaniment to all sorts of fish, poultry and meat dishes.

INGREDIENTS

Serves 4
275g/10oz long grain rice
1 bunch spring onions, finely sliced
1 green pepper, seeded and finely diced
1 yellow pepper, seeded and finely diced
225g/8oz tomatoes, peeled, seeded and chopped
30ml/2 tbsp fresh chopped coriander

For the dressing
75ml/5 tbsp mixed sunflower and olive oil
15ml/1 tbsp rice vinegar
5ml/1 tsp Dijon mustard
salt and ground black pepper

1 Cook the rice for 10–12 minutes until tender but still slightly firm. Do not overcook. Drain and rinse with cold water.

2 Allow the rice to cool completely and then place in a large serving bowl. Add the spring onions, peppers, tomatoes and coriander.

3 Make the dressing by putting all the ingredients in a jar with a tight-fitting lid and shaking vigorously until well blended. Stir the dressing into the rice and adjust the seasoning.

4 Cover and chill for about 1 hour before serving.

— COOK'S TIP —

Cooked garden peas, cooked diced carrot and/or canned or frozen sweetcorn could be added to this adaptable salad.

— NUTRITION NOTES —

Per portion:
Energy	275kcals/1162kJ
Protein	4.3g
Fat	11.1g
Saturated fat	1.8g
Carbohydrate	42g
Sugar	2.8g
Fibre (NSP)	1.6g
Calcium	37mg

FREE FROM

Salad Niçoise

There are probably as many versions of this salad as there are cooks in Provence. This regional classic makes a wonderful lunch or starter to a main meal.

INGREDIENTS

Serves 4

225g/8oz French beans, trimmed
450g/1lb new potatoes, peeled and cut
    into 2.5cm/1in pieces
white wine vinegar and olive oil,
    for sprinkling
1 small cos or round lettuce
4 ripe plum tomatoes, quartered
1 small cucumber, peeled, seeded
    and sliced
1 green or red pepper, thinly sliced
4 eggs, hard-boiled, peeled
    and quartered
24 black olives
225g/8oz can tuna in brine, drained
50g/2oz can anchovies, drained
basil leaves, to garnish

For the dressing

15ml/1 tbsp Dijon mustard
50g/2oz can anchovies, drained
1 garlic clove, crushed
60ml/4 tbsp lemon juice
120ml/4fl oz/½ cup sunflower oil
120ml/4fl oz/½ cup extra virgin
    olive oil
salt and ground black pepper

FREE FROM

NUTRITION NOTES

Per portion:

Energy	319kcals/1327kJ
Protein	18.2g
Fat	25.3g
Saturated fat	3.4g
Carbohydrate	4.6g
Sugar	4.3g
Fibre (NSP)	2.3g
Calcium	81mg

---

1 To make the dressing, place the mustard, anchovies and garlic in a bowl and blend together by pressing the garlic and anchovies against the sides of the bowl. Season generously with pepper. Using a small whisk, blend in the lemon juice or wine vinegar. Slowly whisk in the sunflower oil in a thin stream and then the olive oil, whisking until the dressing is smooth and creamy.

2 Tip the French beans into a saucepan of salted boiling water and cook for 3 minutes until tender, yet crisp. Transfer to a colander with a slotted spoon then rinse under cold running water. Drain again and set aside.

3 Add the potatoes to the same boiling water, reduce the heat and simmer for 10-15 minutes until just tender, then drain. Sprinkle with a little vinegar and olive oil and a spoonful of the dressing.

4 Arrange the lettuce on a platter, top with the tomatoes, cucumber and pepper, then add the cooked French beans and potatoes.

5 Arrange the eggs, olives, tuna and anchovies on top, distributing them evenly, and garnish with the basil leaves. Drizzle the remaining dressing over the top.

Greek Salad

Use a soya-based alternative to feta cheese if preferred.

INGREDIENTS

Serves 6

1 small cos lettuce, sliced
450g/1lb tomatoes, cut into eighths
1 cucumber, seeded and chopped
200g/7oz feta cheese, crumbled
4 spring onions, sliced
50g/2oz/½ cup black olives, pitted
   and halved

For the dressing
90ml/6 tbsp extra virgin olive oil
25ml/1½ tbsp lemon juice
salt and ground black pepper

1 Put the lettuce, tomatoes, cucumber, feta cheese, spring onions and olives into a large bowl.

2 To make the dressing, whisk together the olive oil and lemon juice, then season with salt and pepper.

3 Pour the dressing over the salad. Toss gently until the ingredients are lightly coated in the dressing, then serve immediately.

NUTRITION NOTES	
Per portion:	
Energy	215kcals/890kJ
Protein	6.6g
Fat	19.1g
Saturated fat	6.4g
Carbohydrate	4.3g
Sugar	4.2g
Fibre (NSP)	1.8g
Calcium	148mg

Spiced Aubergine Salad

This Middle Eastern style salad can be served with warm pitta bread as a starter or light lunch dish or to accompany a main course rice pilaff. Choose the type of yogurt that will suit your diet, or omit it altogether.

INGREDIENTS

Serves 4

2 small aubergines, sliced
75ml/5 tbsp olive oil
50ml/2fl oz/¼ cup red wine vinegar
2 garlic cloves, crushed
15ml/1 tbsp lemon juice
2.5ml/½ tsp ground cumin
2.5ml/½ tsp ground coriander
½ cucumber, thinly sliced
2 tomatoes, thinly sliced
30ml/2 tbsp natural yogurt, to serve
   (optional)
salt and ground black pepper
chopped flat leaf parsley, to garnish

1 Preheat the grill. Brush the aubergine slices lightly with some of the oil and cook under a high heat, turning once, until golden and tender.

2 Cut the cooked aubergine slices into quarters.

3 Mix together the remaining oil, vinegar, garlic, lemon juice, cumin and coriander. Season with salt and pepper and mix thoroughly. Add the warm aubergines, stir well and chill for at least 2 hours.

4 Add the cucumber and tomatoes and mix well. Transfer to a serving dish and spoon the yogurt on top, if using.

NUTRITION NOTES	
Per portion:	
Energy	148kcals/612kJ
Protein	1.5g
Fat	14.2g
Saturated fat	2.11g
Carbohydrate	3.8g
Sugar	3.6g
Fibre (NSP)	1.92g
Calcium	29.7mg

Black and Orange Salad

FREE FROM

The darkness of the olives contrasts with the brightness of the orange wedges in this attractive salad.

INGREDIENTS

Serves 4
3 oranges
115g/4oz/1 cup black olives, pitted
15ml/1 tbsp chopped fresh coriander
15ml/1 tbsp chopped fresh parsley
30ml/2 tbsp olive oil
15ml/1 tbsp lemon juice
2.5ml/ ½ tsp paprika
2.5ml/ ½ tsp ground cumin

1 Cut away the peel and pith from the oranges and cut into wedges.

2 Place the oranges in a salad bowl and add the black olives, coriander and parsley.

3 Blend together the olive oil, lemon juice, paprika and cumin. Pour the dressing over the salad and toss gently. Chill for about 30 minutes and serve.

NUTRITION NOTES	
Per portion:	
Energy	120kcals/500kJ
Protein	1.5g
Fat	8.8g
Saturated fat	1.3g
Carbohydrate	9.2g
Sugar	9.2g
Fibre (NSP)	2.7g
Calcium	69mg

Rocket and Coriander Salad

FREE FROM

Rocket leaves have a wonderful, peppery flavour and, mixed with coriander, make a delicious green salad. However, unless you grow your own rocket, or have access to a plentiful supply, you may well have to use extra spinach or another green leaf in order to pad this salad out.

INGREDIENTS

Serves 4
115g/4oz or more rocket leaves
115g/4oz young spinach leaves
1 large bunch (about 25g/1oz)
  fresh coriander, chopped
2–3 fresh parsley sprigs, chopped
1 garlic clove, crushed
45ml/3 tbsp olive oil
10ml/2 tsp white wine vinegar
pinch of paprika
cayenne pepper
salt

1 Place the rocket and spinach leaves in a salad bowl. Add the chopped coriander and parsley.

2 In a small jug, blend together the garlic, olive oil, vinegar, paprika, cayenne pepper and salt.

3 Pour the dressing over the salad, toss lightly, then serve immediately.

NUTRITION NOTES	
Per portion:	
Energy	88kcals/364kJ
Protein	1.6g
Fat	8.7g
Saturated fat	1.2g
Carbohydrate	0.9g
Sugar	0.8g
Fibre (NSP)	1.2g
Calcium	97mg

MEAT AND POULTRY

Whether your preference is for lamb, beef, pork or chicken you're bound to find a recipe here to please. From exotic Middle Eastern Lamb Tagine, subtly flavoured with spices, through deliciously rich Beef Rolls with Garlic and Tomato Sauce, to simple but succulent Spiced Grilled Poussins, there are dishes to suit every taste and time of year. Pork Fillet with Sage and Orange makes a speedy mid-week supper, while Spiced Duck with Pears is the perfect choice for guests.

Lamb Tagine

INGREDIENTS

Serves 4

115g/4oz/ ½ cup dried apricots
30ml/2 tbsp olive oil
1 large onion, chopped
1kg/2¼lb boneless shoulder of
  lamb, cubed
5ml/1 tsp ground cumin
5ml/1 tsp ground coriander
5ml/1 tsp ground cinnamon
grated rind and juice of ½ orange
5ml/1 tsp saffron strands
15ml/1 tbsp ground almonds
about 300ml/ ½ pint/1¼ cups lamb or
  chicken stock
15ml/1 tbsp sesame seeds
salt and ground black pepper
fresh parsley, to garnish
couscous, to serve

1 Cut the apricots in half and put in a bowl with 150ml/ ¼ pint/⅔ cup water. Leave to soak overnight.

2 Preheat the oven to 180°C/350°F/ Gas 4. Heat the olive oil in a flameproof casserole. Add the onion and cook gently for 10 minutes until soft and golden.

3 Stir in the lamb. Add the cumin, coriander and cinnamon, with salt and pepper to taste. Stir to coat the lamb cubes in the spices, then cook, stirring, for 5 minutes.

4 Add the apricots and their soaking liquid. Stir in the orange rind and juice, saffron, ground almonds and enough stock to cover. Cover the casserole and cook in the oven for 1–1½ hours until the meat is tender, stirring occasionally and adding extra stock, if necessary.

5 Meanwhile, heat a heavy-based frying pan, add the sesame seeds and dry fry, shaking the pan, until the seeds are golden. Sprinkle the sesame seeds over the meat, garnish with parsley and serve with couscous.

--- COOK'S TIP ---

Substitute rice for the couscous and this dish will be both wheat- and gluten-free.

--- NUTRITION NOTES ---

Per portion:

Energy	598kcals/2504kJ
Protein	56g
Fat	35g
Saturated fat	12.1g
Carbohydrate	14.2g
Sugar	13.6g
Fibre (NSP)	3.4g
Calcium	111mg

Lamb Pie with Mustard Thatch

INGREDIENTS

Serves 4

800g/1¾lb floury potatoes, diced
15ml/1 tbsp wholegrain mustard
a little pure vegetable margarine
450g/1lb minced lean lamb
1 onion, chopped
2 celery sticks, thinly sliced
2 carrots, diced
30ml/2 tbsp cornflour
150ml/¼ pint/⅔ cup beef stock
15ml/1 tbsp vegetarian Worcestershire
  sauce
30ml/2 tbsp chopped fresh rosemary,
  or 10ml/2 tsp dried
salt and ground black pepper
fresh vegetables, to serve

FREE FROM

1 Cook the potatoes in boiling lightly salted water until tender. Drain well and mash until smooth, then stir in the mustard, margarine and seasoning to taste. Meanwhile, preheat the oven to 200°C/400°F/Gas 6.

2 Fry the lamb in a non-stick pan, breaking it up with a fork, until lightly browned. Add the onion, celery and carrots to the pan and cook for 2–3 minutes, stirring.

3 Blend together the cornflour and stock and stir into the lamb mixture. Bring to the boil, stirring, then remove from the heat. Add the Worcestershire sauce and rosemary and season with salt and pepper.

4 Transfer the lamb mixture to a 1.75 litre/3 pint/7½ cup ovenproof dish and spread the potato topping over evenly, swirling with the edge of a knife. Bake for 30–35 minutes until golden. Serve hot with fresh vegetables.

NUTRITION NOTES	
Per portion:	
Energy	371kcals/1559kJ
Protein	28g
Fat	13.7g
Saturated fat	6.8g
Carbohydrate	36g
Sugar	4.5g
Fibre (NSP)	3.5g
Calcium	177mg

——— COOK'S TIP ———

Vegetarian Worcestershire sauce, which doesn't contain anchovies, is available from health food shops.

Green Peppercorn and Cinnamon Crusted Lamb

FREE
FROM

Racks of lamb are perfect for dinner parties. This version has a spiced crumb coating.

INGREDIENTS

Serves 6
50g/2oz ciabatta bread
15ml/1 tbsp drained green peppercorns
    in brine, lightly crushed
15ml/1 tbsp ground cinnamon
1 garlic clove, crushed
2.5ml/½ tsp salt
25g/1oz/2 tbsp pure vegetable
    margarine, melted
10ml/2 tsp Dijon mustard
2 racks of lamb, trimmed
400ml/14fl oz/1⅔ cups lamb stock
30ml/2 tbsp tomato purée
fresh vegetables, to serve

1 Preheat the oven to 220°C/425°F/ Gas 7. Break the ciabatta bread into pieces, spread out on a baking sheet and bake for about 10 minutes or until pale golden. Leave to cool, then process the bread in a blender or food processor to make fine crumbs.

2 Tip the crumbs into a bowl and add the green peppercorns, cinnamon, garlic and salt. Stir in the melted margarine. Spread the mustard over the lamb. Press the crumb mixture on to the mustard to make a thin, even crust. Put the racks in a roasting tin and roast for 30 minutes, covering the ends with foil if they start to brown too quickly.

3 Remove the lamb to a carving dish, cover with loosely tented foil and keep hot.

4 Skim the fat off the juices in the roasting tin. Stir in the stock and tomato purée. Bring to the boil, stirring in any sediment, then lower the heat and simmer until reduced to a rich gravy. Carve the lamb and serve with the gravy and vegetables.

— NUTRITION NOTES —	
Per portion:	
Energy	414kcals/1983kJ
Protein	53.1g
Fat	27.0g
Saturated fat	11.3g
Carbohydrate	3.1g
Sugar	1.1g
Fibre (NSP)	1.5g
Calcium	26mg

Lamb Casserole with Garlic and Broad Beans

This Spanish-influenced recipe makes a substantial meal, served with creamed potatoes.

INGREDIENTS

Serves 6

45ml/3 tbsp olive oil
1.5kg/3–3½lb fillet lamb, cut into
   5cm/2in cubes
1 large onion, chopped
6 large garlic cloves, unpeeled
1 bay leaf
5ml/1 tsp paprika
120ml/4fl oz/½ cup lamb stock
115g/4oz shelled fresh or frozen
   broad beans
30ml/2 tbsp chopped fresh parsley
salt and ground black pepper

1 Heat 30ml/2 tbsp of the oil in a large frying pan. Add half the meat and brown well on all sides. Transfer to a plate. Brown the rest of the meat in the same way and remove from the pan.

2 Heat the remaining oil in a large saucepan, add the onion and cook for about 5 minutes, until soft. Add the meat and mix well.

3 Add the garlic cloves, bay leaf, paprika and stock. Season with salt and pepper. Bring to the boil, then cover and simmer very gently for 1½–2 hours, until the meat is tender.

4 Add the broad beans about 10 minutes before the end of the cooking time. Stir in the parsley just before serving.

NUTRITION NOTES

Per portion:	
Energy	414kcals/1983kJ
Protein	53.1g
Fat	27g
Saturated fat	11.3g
Carbohydrate	3.1g
Sugar	1.1g
Fibre (NSP)	1.5g
Calcium	26mg

COOK'S TIP

Use canned beans, such as haricot or flageolet, instead of broad beans.

FREE FROM

Turkish Lamb Pilau

INGREDIENTS

Serves 4

45ml/3 tbsp pure vegetable oil
1 large onion, finely chopped
450g/1lb lamb fillet, cut into
    small cubes
2.5ml/½ tsp ground cinnamon
30ml/2 tbsp tomato purée
45ml/3 tbsp chopped fresh parsley
115g/4oz/½ cup ready-to-eat dried
    apricots, halved
450g/1lb long grain rice, rinsed
75g/3oz/¾ cup pistachio nuts,
    chopped (optional)
salt and ground black pepper
flat leaf parsley, to garnish

1 Heat the oil in a large heavy-based pan. Add the onion and cook until golden. Add the lamb and brown on all sides, then stir in the cinnamon, salt and pepper. Cover and cook gently for 10 minutes.

2 Add the tomato purée and enough water to cover the meat. Stir in the parsley, then bring to the boil. Cover the pan and simmer very gently for 1½ hours, until the meat is tender.

3 Add enough water to the pan to make up to about 600ml/1 pint/2½ cups liquid. Add the apricots and rice and stir in the pistachio nuts, if using.

4 Bring to the boil, cover tightly and simmer for about 20 minutes, until the rice is cooked. (You may have to add a little more water, if necessary.) Transfer to a warmed serving dish and garnish with parsley before serving.

NUTRITION NOTES	
Per portion:	
Energy	740kcals/3129kJ
Protein	33.1g
Fat	22.3g
Saturated fat	9.3g
Carbohydrate	108g
Sugar	11.8g
Fibre (NSP)	2.5g
Calcium	92mg

Pork-stuffed Cabbage Parcels

Served with rice, these attractive, tied parcels make a tasty meal.

INGREDIENTS

Serves 4
4 dried Chinese mushrooms, soaked in
   hot water until soft
50g/2oz cellophane noodles, soaked in
   hot water until soft
450g/1lb minced pork
4 spring onions, finely chopped, plus
   4 spring onions to tie the parcels
2 garlic cloves, finely chopped
30ml/2 tbsp fish sauce
12 large outer green cabbage leaves
30ml/2 tbsp vegetable oil
1 small onion, finely chopped
2 garlic cloves, crushed
400g/14oz can plum tomatoes
pinch of sugar
salt and ground black pepper

1 Drain the mushrooms, remove and discard the stems and coarsely chop the caps. Put them in a bowl.

2 Drain the noodles and cut them into short lengths. Add the noodles to the bowl with the pork, chopped spring onions and garlic. Season with the fish sauce and add pepper to taste.

3 Cut off the stem from each cabbage leaf. Blanch the leaves in batches in a saucepan of boiling salted water for about 1 minute. Remove from the pan and refresh under cold water. Drain and dry on kitchen paper. Add the whole spring onions to the boiling water and blanch in the same fashion. Drain well.

4 Fill one of the cabbage leaves with a generous spoonful of the pork and noodle filling. Roll up the leaf sufficiently to enclose the filling, then tuck in the sides and continue rolling the leaf to make a tight parcel. Make more parcels in the same way.

5 Split each blanched spring onion lengthways into three strands by cutting through the bulb and tearing upwards. Tie each of the cabbage parcels with a length of spring onion.

6 Heat the oil in a large flameproof casserole. Add the onion and garlic and fry for 2 minutes or until soft.

7 In a bowl, mash the tomatoes in their juice with a fork, then stir into the casserole. Season with salt, pepper and a pinch of sugar, then bring to a simmer. Add the cabbage parcels, cover and cook gently for 20–25 minutes or until the filling is cooked. Add a little water if the sauce is too dry.

FREE
FROM

——— NUTRITION NOTES ———	
Per portion:	
Energy	309kcals/1569kJ
Protein	26.5g
Fat	13.9g
Saturated fat	3.4g
Carbohydrate	19.4g
Sugar	5.3g
Fibre (NSP)	2.2g
Calcium	60mg

Pork Fillet with Sage and Orange

Sage is often partnered with pork – there seems to be a natural affinity. The addition of orange brings complexity and balances the sometimes overpowering flavour of sage.

INGREDIENTS

Serves 4

2 pork fillets, about 350g/12oz each
15g/½oz/1 tbsp pure vegetable
    margarine
300ml/ ½ pint/ 1¼ cups well-flavoured
    chicken stock
2 garlic cloves, very finely chopped
grated rind and juice of
    1 unwaxed orange
3 or 4 sage leaves, finely chopped
10ml/2 tsp cornflour or arrowroot
salt and ground black pepper
orange wedges and sage leaves,
    to garnish

1 Season the pork fillets lightly with salt and pepper. Melt the margarine in a heavy flameproof casserole over a medium-high heat, then add the meat and cook for 5–6 minutes, turning to brown all sides evenly.

2 Add the stock, boil for about 1 minute, then add the garlic, orange rind and sage. Bring to the boil; reduce the heat to low, then cover and simmer for 20 minutes, turning once, until the meat can be pierced with a knife. Transfer the pork to a warmed platter; cover.

3 Bring the sauce to the boil. Blend the cornflour or arrowroot and orange juice and stir into the sauce, then boil gently over a medium heat for a few minutes, stirring frequently, until the sauce is slightly thickened. Strain into a gravy boat or serving jug.

4 Slice the pork diagonally and pour the meat juices into the sauce.

5 Arrange the pork slices on warmed plates and spoon a little sauce over the top. Garnish with orange wedges and sage leaves and serve the remaining sauce separately.

NUTRITION NOTES	
Per portion:	
Energy	330kcals/1378kJ
Protein	36.2g
Fat	15.5g
Saturated fat	5.7g
Carbohydrate	2.65g
Sugar	0.3g
Fibre (NSP)	0g
Calcium	16.7mg

Beef Rolls with Garlic and Tomato Sauce

Thin slices of beef are wrapped around a richly flavoured stuffing in this classic Italian recipe.

INGREDIENTS

Serves 4

4 thin slices of rump steak, about
   115g/4oz each
4 slices smoked ham
150g/5oz/1⅔ cups freshly grated
   Parmesan cheese
2 garlic cloves, crushed
75ml/5 tbsp chopped fresh parsley
2 eggs, soft-boiled, shelled and
   chopped (optional)
45ml/3 tbsp olive oil
1 large onion, finely chopped
150ml/¼ pint/⅔ cup passata
2 bay leaves
200ml/7fl oz/scant 1 cup beef stock
salt and ground black pepper
flat leaf parsley, to garnish

1 Preheat the oven to 160°C/325°F/ Gas 3. Place the beef slices on a sheet of greaseproof paper. Cover the beef with another sheet of greaseproof paper or clear film and beat with a mallet or rolling pin until very thin. Place a ham slice over each.

2 Mix the cheese in a bowl with the garlic, parsley, eggs if using, and a little salt and pepper. Stir well until all the ingredients are evenly mixed.

3 Spoon the stuffing on to the ham and beef slices. Fold two opposite sides of the meat over the stuffing, then roll up the meat to form neat parcels. Secure with string.

4 Heat the oil in a frying pan. Add the parcels and fry quickly on all sides to brown. Transfer to an ovenproof dish.

5 Add the onion to the frying pan and fry for 3 minutes. Stir in the passata, bay leaves and stock and season with salt and pepper. Bring to the boil, then pour the sauce over the meat in the dish.

6 Cover the dish and bake for 1 hour. Lift the beef rolls out of the pan using a draining spoon and remove the string. Transfer to warm serving plates.

7 Taste the sauce, season with salt and pepper if necessary, and spoon it over the meat. Serve garnished with flat leaf parsley.

FREE FROM

NUTRITION NOTES

Per portion:

Energy	490kcals/2049kJ
Protein	53.5g
Fat	28.1g
Saturated fat	12g
Carbohydrate	2.9g
Sugar	2.3g
Fibre (NSP)	0.6g
Calcium	470mg

Spiced Grilled Poussins

FREE FROM

The spice coating keeps the poussins moist as well as giving them a delicious flavour.

INGREDIENTS

Serves 4
2 garlic cloves, roughly chopped
5ml/1 tsp ground cumin
5ml/1 tsp ground coriander
pinch of cayenne pepper
½ small onion, chopped
60ml/4 tbsp olive oil
2.5ml/ ½ tsp salt
2 poussins
lemon wedges, to garnish

VARIATION

Chicken portions and lamb chops can also be cooked in this way.

---

1 Combine the garlic, cumin, coriander, cayenne pepper, onion, olive oil and salt in a food processor. Process to make a paste that will spread smoothly.

2 Cut the poussins in half lengthways. Place them skin-side up in a shallow dish and spread with the spice paste. Cover and leave to marinate in a cool place for 2 hours.

3 Grill or barbecue the poussins for 15–20 minutes, turning them frequently, until cooked and lightly charred on the outside. Serve immediately, garnished with lemon wedges.

NUTRITION NOTES

Per portion:

Energy	239kcals/999kJ
Protein	23.1g
Fat	16.1g
Saturated fat	3.1g
Carbohydrate	0.6g
Sugar	0.4g
Fibre (NSP)	0.1g
Calcium	11mg

Chicken with 40 Cloves of Garlic

FREE FROM

This recipe is not as strong-tasting as it sounds. Long, slow cooking makes the garlic soft and fragrant and the delicate flavour permeates the chicken.

INGREDIENTS

Serves 4
½ lemon
fresh rosemary sprigs
1.5kg/3lb chicken
4 garlic bulbs
60ml/4 tbsp olive oil
salt and ground black pepper
steamed broad beans and spring onions,
   to serve

1 Preheat the oven to 190°C/375°F/ Gas 5. Place the lemon and rosemary in the chicken. Separate three of the garlic bulbs into cloves and remove the husks, but do not peel. Slice the top off the other garlic bulb.

2 Heat the oil in a large flameproof casserole. Add the chicken, turning it in the oil to coat. Season with salt and pepper and add all the garlic.

3 Cover the casserole with foil, then the lid, to seal well. Cook in the oven for 1–1¼ hours until the chicken is tender. Remove the chicken and whole garlic from the casserole. Mash the remaining garlic into the pan juices to make a sauce and serve the chicken with the roast garlic and the garlic sauce, accompanied by steamed broad beans and spring onions.

NUTRITION NOTES

Per portion:

Energy	354kcals/1485kJ
Protein	69.7
Fat	26.2
Saturated fat	5.9g
Carbohydrate	4.9g
Sugar	0.5g
Fibre (NSP)	1.23g
Calcium	32mg

Mediterranean Roasted Chicken

This is a delicious alternative to a traditional roast chicken. Use a corn-fed or free-range bird, if available, and choose organic vegetables. This recipe also works well with guinea fowl.

INGREDIENTS

Serves 4
1.75kg/4–4½lb roasting chicken
150ml/¼ pint/⅔ cup extra virgin olive oil
½ lemon
few sprigs of fresh thyme
450g/1lb small new potatoes
1 aubergine, cut into 2.5cm/1in cubes
1 red pepper, seeded and quartered
1 fennel bulb, trimmed and quartered
8 large garlic cloves, unpeeled
coarse salt and ground black pepper

3 Remove the chicken from the oven and season with salt. Turn the chicken right side up, and baste with the juices from the tin.

4 Surround the bird with the new potatoes. the tin juices until coated, and ret tin to the oven and continue roasting for 30 minutes.

7 To find out if the chicken is cooked, push the tip of a sharp knife between the thigh and breast. If the juices run clear, it is done. If not, return the chicken to the oven for about 10 minutes and test again. The vegetables should be tender and just beginning to brown.

8 Serve the chicken and vegetables from the tin, or transfer the vegetables to a serving dish, joint the chicken and place it on top. Serve the skimmed juices in a gravy boat.

1 Preheat the oven to 200°C/400°F/ Gas 6. Rub the chicken all over with some of the extra virgin olive oil and season with pepper.

2 Place the lemon half inside the bird, with a sprig or two of thyme. Put the chicken breast-side down in a large roasting tin. Transfer to the oven and roast for about 30 minutes.

5 Remove the tin from the oven and add the aubergine, red pepper, fennel and garlic cloves. Drizzle with the remaining olive oil, and season with salt and pepper.

6 Add any remaining thyme to the vegetables. Return the tin to the oven, and cook for 30–50 minutes more, basting and turning the vegetables occasionally.

COOK'S TIP

Extra virgin olive oil is the highest quality, obtained by a single cold pressing of the finest olives. It has a pure fruity flavour which makes it ideal for cooking.

NUTRITION NOTES

Per portion:

Energy	724kcals/3040kJ
Protein	70g
Fat	40g
Saturated fat	8.1g
Carbohydrate	22.2g
Sugar	5.4g
Fibre (NSP)	3.72g
Calcium	52mg

Stoved Chicken

"Stovies" were originally – not surprisingly – potatoes slowly cooked on the stove with onions and dripping or butter, until falling to pieces. This version includes a succulent layer of bacon and chicken in the middle.

INGREDIENTS

Serves 4
1kg/2¼ lb baking potatoes, cut into
    5mm/¼in slices
2 large onions, thinly sliced
15ml/1 tbsp chopped fresh thyme
25g/1oz/2 tbsp butter
15ml/1 tbsp pure vegetable oil
2 large bacon slices, chopped
4 large chicken joints, halved
600ml/1 pint/2½ cups chicken stock
1 bay leaf
salt and ground black pepper

1 Preheat the oven to 150°C/300°F/ Gas 2. Arrange a thick layer of half the potato slices in the bottom of a large baking dish, then cover with half the onions. Sprinkle with half of the thyme, and season.

2 Heat the butter and oil in a large heavy-based frying pan, add the bacon and chicken and brown on all sides. Using a slotted spoon, transfer the chicken and bacon to the baking dish. Reserve the fat in the pan.

3 Sprinkle the remaining thyme over the chicken, season with salt and pepper, then cover with the remaining onions, followed by a neat layer of overlapping potato slices. Season well.

4 Pour the stock over the potatoes. Tuck in the bay leaf and brush the potatoes with the reserved fat. Cover and bake for 1–1½ hours until the chicken is tender.

5 Preheat the grill. Uncover the baking dish and grill until the potato is brown and crisp. Remove the bay leaf and serve hot.

NUTRITION NOTES	
Per portion:	
Energy	565kcals/2377kJ
Protein	47g
Fat	22.5g
Saturated fat	8.7g
Carbohydrate	45g
Sugar	3.1g
Fibre (NSP)	3.7g
Calcium	37mg

Spiced Duck with Pears

This delicious casserole is based on a Catalan dish that uses goose or duck. The sautéed pears are added towards the end of cooking, along with picarda sauce, a pounded pine nut and garlic paste that both flavours and thickens.

INGREDIENTS

Serves 6
6 duck portions, either breast or
    leg pieces
15ml/1 tbsp olive oil
1 large onion, thinly sliced
1 cinnamon stick, halved
2 thyme sprigs
475ml/16fl oz/2 cups chicken stock

To finish
3 firm ripe pears
30ml/2 tbsp olive oil
2 garlic cloves, sliced
25g/1oz/⅓ cup pine nuts
2.5ml/½ tsp saffron strands
25g/1oz/2 tbsp raisins
salt and ground black pepper
thyme sprigs or fresh parsley,
    to garnish
mashed potato and a green vegetable
    (optional), to serve

1 Preheat the oven to 180°C/350°F/ Gas 4. Fry the duck portions in the olive oil for about 5 minutes until the skin is golden. Transfer the duck to an ovenproof dish and drain off all but 15ml/1 tbsp of the fat left in the pan.

2 Add the onion to the pan and fry, stirring, for 5 minutes. Add the cinnamon stick, thyme and stock and bring to the boil. Pour over the duck and bake 1¼ hours.

3 Meanwhile, peel, core and halve the pears and fry quickly in the oil until beginning to turn golden on the cut sides. Pound the garlic, pine nuts and saffron in a mortar, with a pestle, to make a thick, smooth paste.

4 Add the garlic and pine nut paste to the casserole along with the raisins and pears. Return the dish to the oven and bake for a further 15 minutes until the pears are tender.

5 Season to taste with salt and pepper and garnish with parsley or thyme. Serve with mashed potatoes and a green vegetable, if you wish.

NUTRITION NOTES	
Per portion:	
Energy	783kcals/3277kJ
Protein	56.5g
Fat	35.7g
Saturated fat	8.3g
Carbohydrate	51.3g
Sugar	57.2g
Fibre (NSP)	7.8g
Calcium	103mg

FREE FROM

FISH AND SEAFOOD

Explore some of the world's cuisines with the fish recipes in this

chapter. From France you can sample Mediterranean Baked Fish;

from Italy you have Fresh Tuna and Tomato Stew. From further

afield, you can try Fish Balls with Chinese Greens and, still in an

Asian mood, there's an Indonesian speciality, Spiced Prawns with

Coconut. All these recipes combine wonderful taste sensations

and bring you delicious and healthy dishes.

Mediterranean Baked Fish

INGREDIENTS

Serves 4

3 potatoes
30ml/2 tbsp olive oil, plus extra
    for drizzling
2 onions, halved and sliced
2 garlic cloves, very finely chopped
675g/1½lb thick skinless fish fillets,
    such as turbot or sea bass
1 bay leaf
1 thyme sprig
3 tomatoes, peeled and thinly sliced
30ml/2 tbsp orange juice
60ml/4 tbsp fish stock
2.5ml/½ tsp saffron threads, steeped in
    60ml/4 tbsp boiling water
salt and ground black pepper

1 Cook the potatoes in boiling salted water for 15 minutes, then drain and allow to cool. When the potatoes are cool enough to handle, peel off the skins and slice them thinly.

— NUTRITION NOTES —

Per portion:

Energy	300kcals/1262kJ
Protein	32.2g
Fat	10.4g
Saturated fat	2.03g
Carbohydrate	17.9g
Sugar	4.7g
Fibre (NSP)	2.1g
Calcium	100mg

2 Meanwhile, heat the olive oil in a heavy-based frying pan and fry the onions over a medium-low heat for about 10 minutes, stirring frequently. Add the garlic and continue cooking for a few minutes until the onions are soft and golden.

3 Preheat the oven to 190°C/375°F/ Gas 5. Layer half the potato slices in a 2 litre/3⅓ pint/8 cup baking dish. Cover with half the onions. Season with salt and pepper.

4 Place the fish fillets on top of the vegetables and tuck the herbs in between them. Top with the tomato slices and then the remaining onions and potatoes.

5 Pour the orange juice, stock and saffron liquid over, season with salt and pepper and drizzle a little extra olive oil on top. Bake, uncovered, for about 30 minutes until the potatoes are tender and the fish is cooked.

Fish with Spinach and Lime

The fish is marinated in a fragrant herb marinade called a *charmoula* in Middle Eastern cooking.

INGREDIENTS

Serves 4

675g/1½lb white fish, such as haddock, cod, sea bass or monkfish
sunflower oil, for frying
500g/1¼lb potatoes, sliced
1 onion, chopped
1–2 garlic cloves, crushed
5 tomatoes, peeled and chopped
375g/12oz fresh spinach, chopped
lime wedges, to garnish

For the *charmoula*
6 spring onions, chopped
10ml/2 tsp fresh thyme
60ml/4 tbsp chopped flat leaf parsley
30ml/2 tbsp chopped fresh coriander
10ml/2 tsp paprika
generous pinch of cayenne pepper
60ml/4 tbsp olive oil
grated rind of 1 lime and 60ml/4 tbsp lime juice
salt

1 Cut the fish into large pieces, discarding any skin and bones, and place in a large shallow dish.

2 Blend together the ingredients for the *charmoula* and season well with salt. Pour over the fish, stir to mix and leave in a cool place, covered with clear film, for 2–4 hours.

3 Heat about 5mm/¼in oil in a large heavy-based pan and fry the potatoes until cooked through and golden. Drain on kitchen paper.

4 Pour off all but about 15ml/1 tbsp of the oil and add the chopped onion, garlic and tomatoes. Cook over a gentle heat for 5–6 minutes, stirring occasionally, until the onion is soft.

5 Place the potatoes on top of the onion and tomato mixture, then add the chopped spinach to the pan.

6 Place the fish on top of the spinach and pour in all the marinade. Cover tightly and cook for 15–18 minutes. After about 8 minutes, carefully stir the contents of the pan so that the fish is distributed evenly throughout the dish. Cover the pan again and continue cooking, but check occasionally – the dish is cooked once the fish is tender and opaque and the spinach has wilted.

7 Serve immediately on individual serving plates, garnished with wedges of lime.

NUTRITION NOTES	
Per portion:	
Energy	369kcals/1549kJ
Protein	36.5g
Fat	13.6g
Saturated fat	2.06g
Carbohydrate	26.3g
Sugar	7.4g
Fibre (NSP)	4.5g
Calcium	174mg

FREE FROM

Fish Balls with Chinese Greens

Tasty fish balls are partnered with a selection of green vegetables to make a fresh and appetizing stir-fry with a Chinese flavour.

INGREDIENTS

Serves 4

450g/1lb white fish fillets, skinned, boned and cubed
3 spring onions, chopped
1 back bacon rasher, chopped
15ml/1 tbsp Chinese rice wine
30ml/2 tbsp tamari
1 egg white

For the vegetables
5ml/1 tsp cornflour or arrowroot
15ml/1 tbsp tamari
150ml/¼ pint/⅔ cup fish stock
30ml/2 tbsp vegetable oil
2 garlic cloves, sliced
2.5cm/1in piece fresh root ginger, cut into thin shreds
75g/3oz green beans
175g/6oz mangetouts
3 spring onions, sliced diagonally into 5–7.5cm/2–3in lengths
1 small head pak choi, stems trimmed and leaves torn
salt and ground black pepper

COOK'S TIP

Tamari is a wheat-free type of soy sauce and can be found in Asian shops. If you are not allergic to wheat, you can subsitute soy sauce, if you prefer.

NUTRITION NOTES

Per portion:

Energy	201kcals/1115kJ
Protein	26.5g
Fat	8.75g
Saturated fat	1.5g
Carbohydrate	3.9g
Sugar	3.2g
Fibre (NSP)	2.2g
Calcium	67mg

1 Put the fish, spring onions, bacon, rice wine, tamari and egg white in a food processor. Process until smooth. With wetted hands, form the mixture into about 24 small balls.

2 Steam the fish balls in batches in a lightly greased bamboo steamer in a wok for 5–10 minutes until firm. Transfer to a plate and keep warm.

3 In a small bowl, blend together the cornflour or arrowroot, tamari and stock until smooth. Set aside.

4 Heat a wok until hot, add the oil and swirl it around. Add the garlic and ginger and stir-fry for 1 minute. Then add the beans and stir-fry for 2–3 minutes, then add the mangetouts, spring onions and pak choi. Stir-fry for 2–3 minutes.

5 Add the stock mixture to the wok and cook, stirring, until it has thickened and the vegetables are tender but still crisp. Taste, and adjust the seasoning, if necessary. Serve at once with the steamed fish balls.

Tuna with Pan-fried Tomatoes

INGREDIENTS

Serves 2

2 tuna steaks, about 175g/6oz each
90ml/6 tbsp olive oil
30ml/2 tbsp lemon juice
2 garlic cloves, chopped
5ml/1 tsp chopped fresh thyme
4 canned anchovy fillets, drained and
    finely chopped
225g/8oz plum tomatoes, halved
30ml/2 tbsp chopped fresh parsley
4–6 black olives, pitted and chopped
ground black pepper
crusty bread, to serve (optional)

1 Place the tuna steaks in a shallow
non-metallic dish. Mix 60ml/
4 tbsp of the oil with the lemon juice,
garlic, thyme, anchovies and pepper.
Pour this mixture over the tuna and
leave to marinate in a cool place for
at least 1 hour.

2 Lift the tuna from the marinade
and place on a grill rack. Grill for
4 minutes on each side, or until firm to
the touch, basting with the marinade.
Take care not to overcook.

3 Meanwhile, heat the remaining oil
in a frying pan. Add the tomatoes
and fry for 2 minutes only on each side.

4 Divide the tomatoes equally
between two serving plates and
scatter the chopped parsley and olives
over. Top each with a tuna steak.

5 Add the remaining marinade to the
pan juices and warm through. Pour
over the tomatoes and tuna steaks and
serve at once with crusty bread (if your
diet allows) for mopping up the juices.

NUTRITION NOTES

Per portion:	
Energy	578kcals/2405kJ
Protein	21.8g
Fat	21.6g
Saturated fat	7.2g
Carbohydrate	3.6g
Sugar	3.6g
Fibre (NSP)	1.4g
Calcium	57mg

FREE FROM

Red Mullet with Cumin

INGREDIENTS

FREE FROM

Serves 4
8–12 red mullet, depending on the size
   of the fish
fresh parsley and finely pared strips of
   lemon rind, to garnish

For the marinade
10ml/2 tsp ground cumin
5ml/1 tsp paprika
60ml/4 tbsp lemon juice
45ml/3 tbsp olive oil
30ml/2 tbsp chopped fresh parsley
salt and ground black pepper

For the fresh tomato sauce
5 large tomatoes
2 garlic cloves, chopped
60ml/4 tbsp chopped fresh parsley
   and coriander
30ml/2 tbsp olive oil
30ml/2 tbsp lemon juice

1 Make 2–3 slashes along the sides of
the fish and place them in a shallow
non-metallic dish. Blend together the
ingredients for the marinade and rub
into the fish on both sides. Set aside for
2 hours in a cool place.

2 Make the fresh tomato sauce. Peel
the tomatoes and cut into small
pieces, discarding the core and seeds.
Place in a bowl and stir in the
remaining ingredients. Set aside in the
fridge or a cool place.

3 Heat the grill or prepare the
barbecue. Grill or barbecue the fish
for 3–4 minutes on each side, until the
flesh is tender. Garnish with parsley and
lemon rind and serve immediately with
the fresh tomato sauce.

---- NUTRITION NOTES ----

Per portion:
Energy	334kcals/1399kJ
Protein	33.1g
Fat	21.1g
Saturated fat	2.1g
Carbohydrate	3.65g
Sugar	3.65g
Fibre (NSP)	1.1g
Calcium	130mg

Spicy Fish Brochettes

INGREDIENTS

FREE FROM

Serves 4 as a starter
450g/1lb white fish fillets, such as cod,
   haddock, monkfish or sea bass
olive oil, for brushing
lime wedges and fresh tomato sauce,
   to serve

For the spicy marinade
½ onion, grated or very finely chopped
2 garlic cloves, crushed
30ml/2 tbsp chopped fresh coriander
15ml/1 tbsp chopped fresh parsley
5ml/1 tsp ground cumin
10ml/2 tsp paprika
good pinch of ground ginger
25ml/1½ tbsp white wine vinegar
30ml/2 tbsp lime juice
salt and cayenne pepper

1 First make the marinade. Blend all
the ingredients and season to taste
with salt and cayenne pepper.

2 Cut the fish into 1cm/½in cubes,
discarding the skin and bones.
Place in a shallow non-metallic dish.
Add the marinade and stir to coat the
fish thoroughly. Cover with clear film
and set aside for about 2 hours.

3 Preheat the grill. Thread the fish on
to 12 small or 8 larger metal skewers.
Place on a grill pan and brush with a
little olive oil. Cook the brochettes for
7–10 minutes until the fish is cooked
through, turning and brushing with
more oil occasionally. Serve with
wedges of lime and fresh tomato sauce.

---- NUTRITION NOTES ----

Per portion:
Energy	77kcals/330kJ
Protein	17.7g
Fat	0.4g
Saturated fat	0.1g
Carbohydrate	0.7g
Sugar	0.5g
Fibre (NSP)	0.1g
Calcium	11mg

Halibut with Tomato Vinaigrette

The tomato vinaigrette, an uncooked mixture of tomatoes, aromatic fresh herbs and olive oil, can either be served at room temperature or slightly warm.

INGREDIENTS

Serves 2

3 large ripe beefsteak tomatoes, peeled, seeded and chopped
2 shallots or 1 small red onion, finely chopped
1 garlic clove, crushed
90ml/6 tbsp chopped mixed fresh herbs, such as parsley, coriander, basil, tarragon, chervil or chives
120ml/4fl oz/ ½ cup extra virgin olive oil, plus extra for brushing
4 halibut fillets or steaks, about 175–200g/6–7oz each
salt and ground black pepper
green salad, to serve

1 In a medium bowl, mix together the tomatoes, shallots or onion, garlic and herbs. Stir in the oil and season with salt and ground pepper. Cover the bowl and leave the sauce at room temperature for about 1 hour to allow the flavours to blend.

2 Preheat the grill. Line a grill pan with foil and brush the foil lightly with oil.

3 Season the fish with salt and pepper. Place the fish on the foil and brush with a little extra oil. Grill the fish for 5–6 minutes until the flesh is opaque and the top is lightly browned.

4 Pour the tomato vinaigrette into a saucepan and heat gently for a few minutes. Serve the fish with the sauce and a green salad.

NUTRITION NOTES	
Per portion:	
Energy	652kcals/1360kJ
Protein	44.5g
Fat	49.5g
Saturated fat	7.3g
Carbohydrate	7.2g
Sugar	6.6g
Fibre (NSP)	1.9g
Calcium	90.5mg

Fresh Tuna and Tomato Stew

This tuna stew has a delicious Italian flavour.

INGREDIENTS

Serves 4

12 baby onions, peeled
900g/2lb ripe tomatoes
675g/1½lb fresh tuna
45ml/3 tbsp olive oil
2 garlic cloves, crushed
45ml/3 tbsp chopped fresh herbs
2 bay leaves
2.5ml/ ½ tsp caster sugar
30ml/2 tbsp sun-dried tomato paste
150ml/ ¼ pint/ ⅔ cup fish stock
salt and ground black pepper
baby courgettes and fresh herbs,
   to garnish

1 Leave the onions whole and cook in a pan of boiling water for 4–5 minutes until softened. Drain.

2 Plunge the tomatoes into boiling water for 30 seconds, then rinse in cold water. Peel away the skins and chop the tomatoes roughly.

3 Cut the tuna into 2.5cm/1in chunks. Heat the oil in a large frying or sauté pan and quickly fry the tuna until browned. Transfer the tuna chunks to kitchen paper to drain.

4 Add the onions, garlic, tomatoes, chopped herbs, bay leaves, sugar, tomato paste and stock and bring to the boil, breaking up the tomatoes with a wooden spoon.

5 Reduce the heat and simmer gently for 5 minutes. Return the fish to the sauce in the pan and cook for a further 5 minutes. Season, and serve hot, garnished with baby courgettes and fresh herbs.

COOK'S TIP

The best fresh herbs to use as a garnish for tuna are basil, parsley or chives.

NUTRITION NOTES

Per portion:

Energy	412kcals/1728kJ
Protein	42.5g
Fat	18.7g
Saturated fat	3.7g
Carbohydrate	13.1g
Sugar	11.3g
Fibre (NSP)	3.3g
Calcium	66mg

FREE FROM

Buckwheat Noodles with Smoked Trout

FREE
FROM

These earthy flavours mix perfectly with the crisp pak choi.

INGREDIENTS

Serves 4

350g/12oz buckwheat noodles
30ml/2 tbsp vegetable oil
115g/4oz fresh shiitake
   mushrooms, quartered
2 garlic cloves, finely chopped
15ml/1 tbsp grated fresh root ginger
225g/8oz pak choi
1 spring onion, finely sliced diagonally
15ml/1 tbsp dark sesame oil
30ml/2 tbsp mirin
30ml/2 tbsp tamari
2 smoked trout, skinned and boned
salt and ground back pepper
30ml/2 tbsp coriander leaves and
   10ml/2 tsp sesame seeds, toasted,
   to garnish (optional)

1 Cook the buckwheat noodles in boiling water for 7–10 minutes until just tender or according to the packet instructions.

2 Meanwhile, heat the oil in a large frying pan. Add the mushrooms and cook, stirring, over a medium heat for 3 minutes. Add the garlic, ginger and pak choi, and continue to cook for 2 minutes.

3 Drain the noodles and add them to the mushroom mixture with the spring onion, sesame oil, mirin and tamari. Toss and season with salt and pepper to taste.

4 Break the smoked trout into bite-size pieces. Arrange the noodle mixture on individual serving plates. Place the smoked trout on top of the noodles.

5 Garnish the noodles with coriander leaves and sesame seeds, if you wish, and serve them immediately.

NUTRITION NOTES

Per portion:

Energy	513kcals/2437kJ
Protein	27.2g
Fat	16.7g
Saturated fat	1.5g
Carbohydrate	67.2g
Sugar	2.9g
Fibre (NSP)	3.5g
Calcium	65mg

Spiced Prawns with Coconut

This delicious, fragrant and spicy dish is based on a traditional Indonesian recipe. Serve with a bowl of plain boiled rice.

INGREDIENTS

Serves 3–4

2–3 fresh red chillies, seeded
    and chopped
3 shallots, chopped
1 lemon grass stalk, chopped
2 garlic cloves, chopped
thin sliver of dried shrimp paste
2.5ml/ ½ tsp ground ginger
5ml/1 tsp ground turmeric
5ml/1 tsp ground coriander
15ml/1 tbsp pure vegetable oil
250ml/8fl oz/1 cup water
2 fresh kaffir lime leaves
5ml/1 tsp light brown soft sugar
2 tomatoes, peeled, seeded
    and chopped
250ml/8fl oz/1 cup coconut milk
675g/1½lb large raw prawns, peeled
    and deveined
squeeze of lemon juice
salt, to taste
shredded spring onions and toasted
    flaked coconut, to garnish

FREE FROM

1 In a mortar, pound the chillies, shallots, lemon grass, garlic, shrimp paste, ginger, turmeric and coriander with a pestle until it forms a paste. Alternatively, process the ingredients in a food processor or blender.

--- NUTRITION NOTES ---

Per portion:
Energy	184–246kcals/916–1222kJ
Protein	30–40g
Fat	4.2–5.4g
Saturated fat	0.6–0.8g
Carbohydrate	6.9–9.3g
Sugar	6.3–8.8g
Fibre (NSP)	0.7–0.9g
Calcium	159–212mg

2 Heat a wok until hot, add the oil and swirl it around. Add the spiced paste and stir-fry for about 2 minutes. Pour in the water and add the kaffir lime leaves, sugar and tomatoes. Simmer for 8–10 minutes until most of the liquid has evaporated.

3 Add the coconut milk and prawns and cook gently, stirring, for about 4 minutes until the prawns are pink. Taste and adjust the seasoning with salt and a squeeze of lemon juice. Serve at once, garnished with shredded spring onions and toasted flaked coconut.

VEGETABLES AND VEGETARIAN DISHES

Fresh vegetables are a vital part of an allergy-free diet, and here you

will find a selection of recipes using seasonal vegetables to their best

advantage. Delicious ideas include Middle Eastern Vegetable Stew,

Ratatouille and Roasted Vegetable Salad. Baby vegetables make a

delicious accompaniment in Summer Vegetable Braise, and seasonal

peas and beans enhance Risotto with Spring Vegetables.

Summer Vegetable Braise

Tender, young vegetables are ideal for quick cooking in a minimum of liquid. Use any mixture of your favourite vegetables as long as they are of similar size.

INGREDIENTS

Serves 4

175g/6oz/2½ cups baby carrots
175g/6oz/2 cups sugar-snap peas
    or mangetouts
115g/4oz baby corn cobs
90ml/6 tbsp vegetable stock
10ml/2 tsp lime juice
salt and ground black pepper
chopped fresh parsley and snipped fresh
    chives, to garnish

3 Season the vegetables with salt and pepper to taste, then add the parsley and chives.

4 Cook the vegetables for a few seconds more, stirring them once or twice until the herbs are well mixed, then serve at once.

───── NUTRITION NOTES ─────

Per portion:

Energy	34kcals/143kJ
Protein	2.6g
Fat	0.4g
Saturated fat	0g
Carbohydrate	5.2g
Sugar	4.4g
Fibre (NSP)	2.6g
Calcium	38.7mg

1 Place the carrots, peas and baby corn cobs in a large heavy-based saucepan with the vegetable stock and lime juice. Bring to the boil.

2 Cover the pan and reduce the heat, then simmer for 6–8 minutes, shaking the pan occasionally, until the vegetables are just tender.

Middle Eastern Vegetable Stew

A spiced dish of mixed vegetables that can be served as a side dish or as a vegetarian main course. Children may prefer less chilli.

INGREDIENTS

Serves 4–6
45ml/3 tbsp vegetable or chicken stock
1 green pepper, seeded and sliced
2 courgettes, sliced
2 carrots, sliced
2 celery sticks, sliced
2 potatoes, diced
400g/14oz can chopped tomatoes
5ml/1 tsp chilli powder
30ml/2 tbsp chopped fresh mint
15ml/1 tbsp ground cumin
400g/14oz can chick-peas, drained
salt and ground black pepper
mint leaves, to garnish

1 Heat the stock in a large flameproof casserole until boiling, then add the sliced pepper, courgettes, carrots and celery. Stir over a high heat for 2–3 minutes, until the vegetables are just beginning to soften.

NUTRITION NOTES

Per portion:

Energy	212–141kcals/898–598kJ
Protein	11.2–7.5g
Fat	3.6–2.4g
Saturated fat	0.4–0.3g
Carbohydrate	35.7–23.8g
Sugar	7.2–4.8g
Fibre (NSP)	7.7–5.1g
Calcium	90.5–60.3mg

2 Add the potatoes, tomatoes, chilli powder, mint and cumin. Add the chick-peas and bring to the boil.

--- COOK'S TIP ---

Chick-peas are traditional in this type of Middle Eastern dish but, if you prefer, red kidney beans or haricot beans can be used instead.

3 Reduce the heat, cover the casserole with a lid and simmer for 30 minutes, or until all the vegetables are tender.

4 Season the stew with salt and pepper to taste and serve hot, garnished with mint leaves.

FREE FROM

Ratatouille

This classic combination of the vegetables that grow abundantly in the south of France is infinitely flexible. Use the recipe as a guide for making the most of what you have on hand.

Ingredients

Serves 6
2 aubergines, about 450g/1lb total, cut into 2cm/¾in slices
60–75ml/4–5 tbsp olive oil
1 large onion, halved and sliced
2 or 3 garlic cloves, very finely chopped
1 large red or yellow pepper, seeded and cut into thin strips
2 large courgettes, cut into 1cm/½in slices
675g/1½lb ripe tomatoes, peeled, seeded and chopped, or 400g/14oz can chopped tomatoes
5ml/1 tsp dried mixed herbs
salt and ground black pepper

COOK'S TIP

Roasting the pepper not only allows you to remove the skin, it adds a delicious, smoky flavour to the ratatouille. Quarter the pepper and grill, skin-side up, until blackened. Enclose the pepper in a sturdy polythene bag and set aside until cool. Peel off the skin, then remove the core and seeds and cut the pepper into strips. Add to the mixture with the cooked aubergine.

NUTRITION NOTES

Per portion:	
Energy	95kcals/396kJ
Protein	1.9g
Fat	7.7g
Saturated fat	1.2g
Carbohydrate	7.4g
Sugar	4.3g
Fibre (NSP)	1.9g
Calcium	28mg

1 Preheat the grill. Brush the aubergine slices with oil on both sides. Grill until lightly browned, turning once, then cut into chunks.

2 Heat 15ml/1 tbsp of the olive oil in a large flameproof casserole and cook the onion for about 10 minutes until lightly golden, stirring frequently. Add the garlic, pepper and courgettes and cook for a further 10 minutes.

3 Add the tomatoes, aubergine, dried herbs and salt and pepper. Simmer gently, covered, over a low heat for about 20 minutes, stirring occasionally. Uncover and continue cooking for a further 20–25 minutes, stirring occasionally, until all the vegetables are tender and the cooking liquid has thickened slightly. Serve hot or at room temperature, if you prefer.

Risotto with Spring Vegetables

This is one of the prettiest risottos, especially if you can get yellow courgettes.

INGREDIENTS

Serves 4

150g/5oz/1 cup shelled fresh peas
115g/4oz/1 cup French beans, cut into
    short lengths
30ml/2 tbsp olive oil
75g/3oz/6 tbsp butter
2 small yellow courgettes, cut
    into matchsticks
1 onion, finely chopped
275g/10oz/1½ cups risotto rice
120ml/4fl oz/½ cup Italian dry
    white vermouth (optional)
about 1 litre/1¾ pints/4 cups boiling
    chicken stock
75g/3oz/1 cup grated Parmesan cheese
a small handful of fresh basil leaves,
    finely shredded, plus a few whole
    leaves, to garnish
salt and ground black pepper

1 Blanch the peas and beans in a large saucepan of lightly salted boiling water for 2–3 minutes until just tender. Drain, refresh under cold running water, drain and set aside.

2 Heat the oil and 25g/1oz/2 tbsp of the butter in a medium saucepan until foaming. Add the courgettes and cook gently for 2–3 minutes or until just softened. Remove the courgettes with a slotted spoon and set aside. Add the onion to the pan and cook gently for about 3 minutes, stirring frequently, until softened.

3 Stir in the rice until the grains start to swell and burst, then add the vermouth, if using. Stir until the vermouth stops sizzling and most of it has been absorbed by the rice, then add a few ladlefuls of the stock, with salt and pepper to taste. Stir over low heat until the stock has been absorbed.

4 Continue cooking and stirring for 20–25 minutes, adding the remaining stock a few ladlefuls at a time. The rice should be *al dente* and the risotto should have a moist and creamy appearance. Gently stir in the vegetables and the remaining butter.

5 Stir in half the Parmesan. Heat through, then stir in the shredded basil and taste for seasoning. Garnish with basil leaves and serve with the remaining Parmesan handed separately.

NUTRITION NOTES	
Per portion:	
Energy	602kcals/2500kJ
Protein	17.2g
Fat	28.9g
Saturated fat	15g
Carbohydrate	59.3g
Sugar	3.9g
Fibre (NSP)	2.9g
Calcium	272mg

Stuffed Vine Leaves

FREE
FROM

A traditional Greek recipe that comes in many guises. This vegetarian version is richly flavoured with fresh herbs, lemon and a little chilli. Serve as a starter or vegetarian main course or as part of a buffet spread.

Ingredients

Serves 6

225g/8oz packet preserved vine
   leaves, drained
1 onion, finely chopped
½ bunch of spring onions,
   finely chopped
60ml/4 tbsp chopped fresh flat
   leaf parsley
10 large mint sprigs, chopped
finely grated rind of 1 lemon
2.5ml/½ tsp crushed dried chillies
7.5ml/1½ tsp fennel seeds, crushed
175g/6oz/scant 1 cup long grain rice
120ml/4fl oz/½ cup extra virgin
   olive oil
salt
lemon wedges and mint leaves, to
   garnish (optional)

1 Rinse the vine leaves in plenty of cold water. Put in a bowl, cover with boiling water and leave for 10 minutes. Drain thoroughly.

2 In a bowl, mix together the onion, spring onions, parsley, mint, lemon rind, chilli, fennel seeds, rice and 25ml/1½ tbsp of the olive oil. Mix thoroughly and season with salt.

3 Place a vine leaf, veined side facing upwards, on a work surface and cut off any stalk. Place a heaped teaspoonful of the rice mixture near the stalk end of the leaf.

4 Fold the stalk end of the leaf over the rice filling, then fold over the sides and carefully roll up into a neat cigar shape.

5 Repeat with the remaining filling to make about 28 stuffed leaves. If some of the vine leaves are quite small, use two and patch them together to make parcels of the same size.

6 Place any remaining leaves in the base of a large heavy-based saucepan. Pack the stuffed leaves in a single layer in the pan. Spoon the remaining oil over then add about 300ml/½ pint/1¼ cups boiling water.

7 Place a small plate over the leaves to keep them submerged in the water. Cover the pan and cook on a very low heat for 45 minutes.

8 Transfer the stuffed leaves to a serving plate and garnish with lemon wedges and mint, if you like.

Cook's Tip

To check that the rice is cooked, lift out one stuffed leaf and cut in half. The rice should have expanded and softened to make a firm parcel. If necessary, cook the stuffed leaves a little longer, adding boiling water if the pan is becoming dry.

Nutrition Notes

Per portion:

Energy	256kcals/1072kJ
Protein	3.9g
Fat	15.8g
Saturated fat	2.3g
Carbohydrate	26.3g
Sugar	1.6g
Fibre (NSP)	0.5g
Calcium	170mg

Green Beans with Tomatoes

This is a real summer favourite using the best ripe plum tomatoes and French beans.

INGREDIENTS

Serves 4

30ml/2 tbsp olive oil
1 large onion, finely sliced
2 garlic cloves, finely chopped
6 large ripe plum tomatoes, peeled, seeded and coarsely chopped
150ml/ ¼ pint/⅔ cup vegetable stock
450g/1lb French green beans, sliced in half lengthways
16 pitted black olives
10ml/2 tsp lemon juice
salt and ground black pepper

1 Heat the oil in a large frying pan. Add the onion and garlic and cook for about 5 minutes until softened.

2 Add the chopped tomatoes, stock, beans, olives and lemon juice and cook over a gentle heat for a further 20 minutes, stirring from time to time, until the sauce is thickened and the beans are tender. Season with salt and pepper to taste and serve at once.

—— COOK'S TIP ——

French beans need little preparation and now that they are grown without the string you simply top and tail them. When buying make sure that the beans snap easily – this is a good sign of freshness.

—— NUTRITION NOTES ——

Per portion:

Energy	140kcals/584kJ
Protein	3.3g
Fat	7.7g
Saturated fat	1.2g
Carbohydrate	7.98g
Sugar	7.38g
Fibre (NSP)	4.3g
Calcium	63mg

Polenta with Mushroom Sauce

Polenta, made from corn, forms the starchy base for many Italian dishes. Its subtle taste works well with the rich mushroom sauce.

INGREDIENTS

Serves 4

1.2 litres/2 pints/5 cups vegetable stock
350g/12oz/3 cups polenta
50g/2oz/⅔ cup grated
  Parmesan cheese
salt and ground black pepper

For the sauce

15g/½oz/1 cup dried
  porcini mushrooms
15ml/1 tbsp olive oil
50g/2oz/¼ cup pure
  vegetable margarine
1 onion, finely chopped
1 carrot, finely chopped
1 celery stick, finely chopped
2 garlic cloves, crushed
450g/1lb/6 cups mixed chestnut
  and large flat mushrooms,
  roughly chopped
120ml/4fl oz/½ cup vegetable stock
400g/14oz can chopped tomatoes
15ml/1 tbsp tomato purée
15ml/1 tbsp chopped fresh
  thyme leaves

1 Make the sauce. Put the dried mushrooms in a bowl, add 150ml/¼ pint/⅔ cup hot water and soak for 20 minutes. Drain the mushrooms, reserving the liquid, and chop them roughly.

NUTRITION NOTES

Per portion:	
Energy	550kcals/2293kJ
Protein	17.2g
Fat	21.3g
Saturated fat	7.6g
Carbohydrate	68.4g
Sugar	5g
Fibre (NSP)	3.1g
Calcium	201mg

---

2 Heat the oil and margarine in a saucepan and add the onion, carrot, celery and garlic. Cook over a low heat for about 5 minutes until the vegetables are beginning to soften, then raise the heat and add the fresh and soaked dried mushrooms to the pan of vegetables. Cook for 8–10 minutes until the mushrooms are softened and golden.

3 Add the stock and boil for 2–3 minutes until reduced, then add the tomatoes and mushroom liquid. Stir in the tomato purée, thyme and salt and pepper. Lower the heat and simmer for 20 minutes until the sauce thickens.

4 Meanwhile, heat the stock for the polenta in a large heavy saucepan. Add a generous pinch of salt. As soon as it simmers, tip in the polenta in a fine stream, whisking until the mixture is smooth. Cook for 30 minutes, stirring constantly, until the polenta comes away from the pan. Remove from the heat and stir in half the Parmesan and some black pepper.

5 Divide the cooked polenta among four heated bowls and top each with the mushroom sauce. Sprinkle with the remaining Parmesan and serve at once.

Cauliflower with Tomatoes and Cumin

This makes an excellent side dish to serve with barbecued or grilled meat or fish.

INGREDIENTS

Serves 4
30ml/2 tbsp sunflower or olive oil
1 onion, chopped
1 garlic clove, crushed
1 small cauliflower, broken into florets
5ml/1 tsp cumin seeds
a good pinch of ground ginger
4 tomatoes, peeled, seeded and quartered
15–30ml/1–2 tbsp lemon juice (optional)
30ml/2 tbsp chopped fresh coriander (optional)
salt and ground black pepper

1 Heat the oil in a flameproof casserole, add the onion and garlic and fry for 2–3 minutes until the onion is softened. Add the cauliflower and fry, stirring, for a further 2–3 minutes until the cauliflower is flecked with brown. Add the cumin seeds and ginger, fry briskly for 1 minute, and then add the tomatoes, 175ml/6fl oz/¾ cup water and some salt and pepper.

2 Bring to the boil and then reduce the heat, cover and simmer for 6–7 minutes, until the cauliflower is just tender.

3 Stir in a little lemon juice to sharpen the flavour, if liked, and adjust the seasoning. Scatter over the coriander, if using, and serve at once.

NUTRITION NOTES	
Per portion:	
Energy	86kcals/358kJ
Protein	2.5g
Fat	6.2g
Saturated fat	0.9g
Carbohydrate	5.3g
Sugar	4.7g
Fibre (NSP)	1.9g
Calcium	20mg

Roasted Vegetable Salad

Oven roasting brings out all the flavours of these classic Mediterranean vegetables. Serve them hot with grilled or roast meat or fish.

INGREDIENTS

Serves 4
2–3 courgettes
1 Spanish onion
2 red peppers
16 cherry tomatoes
2 garlic cloves, chopped
pinch of cumin seeds
5ml/1 tsp fresh thyme or 4–5 torn basil leaves
60ml/4 tbsp olive oil
juice of ½ lemon
5–10ml/1–2 tsp chilli or Tabasco sauce
fresh thyme sprigs, to garnish

1 Preheat the oven to 220°C/425°F/ Gas 7. Top and tail the courgettes and cut into long strips. Cut the onion into thin wedges then cut the red peppers into chunks, discarding the seeds and core.

2 Place the vegetables in a roasting tin, add the tomatoes, garlic, cumin and thyme. Sprinkle with the oil and toss to coat.

3 Cook in the oven for 25–30 minutes until the vegetables are very soft and slightly charred.

4 Blend the lemon juice with the chilli or Tabasco sauce and stir into the vegetables. Garnish with thyme and serve.

NUTRITION NOTES	
Per portion:	
Energy	151kcals/623kJ
Protein	2.8g
Fat	11.8g
Saturated fat	1.7g
Carbohydrate	8.7g
Sugar	7.8g
Fibre (NSP)	2.5g
Calcium	39mg

Red-cooked Tofu with Chinese Mushrooms

Red-cooked is a term applied to Chinese dishes cooked with dark soy sauce. Tamari is a type of soy sauce available in Asian shops that is wheat free.

INGREDIENTS

Serves 4 as a side dish
225g/8oz firm tofu
45ml/3 tbsp tamari
30ml/2 tbsp Chinese rice wine or
    medium-dry sherry
10ml/2 tsp soft dark brown sugar
1 garlic clove, crushed
15ml/1 tbsp grated fresh root ginger
2.5ml/½ tsp Chinese five-spice powder
pinch of ground, roasted
    Szechuan peppercorns
6 dried Chinese black mushrooms
5ml/1 tsp cornflour
30ml/2 tbsp pure vegetable oil
5–6 spring onions, white and green
    parts separated, sliced into 2.5cm/
    1in lengths
small basil leaves, to garnish
rice noodles, to serve

1 Drain the tofu, pat dry with kitchen paper and cut into 2.5cm/1in cubes. Place in a shallow dish.

2 In a small bowl, mix together the tamari, rice wine or sherry, sugar, garlic, ginger, five-spice powder and Szechuan peppercorns. Pour the marinade over the tofu, toss well and leave to marinate for about 30 minutes. Drain, reserving the marinade.

3 Meanwhile, soak the dried black mushrooms in warm water for 20–30 minutes until soft. Drain, reserving 90ml/6 tbsp of the soaking liquid. Squeeze out any excess liquid from the mushrooms, remove the tough stalks and slice the caps. In a small bowl, blend the cornflour with the reserved marinade and mushroom soaking liquid.

4 Heat a wok until hot, add the oil and swirl it around to coat the pan. Add the tofu and fry for 2–3 minutes until evenly golden. Remove from the wok and set aside.

5 Add the mushrooms and white parts of the spring onions to the wok and stir-fry for 2 minutes. Pour in the marinade mixture and stir for 1 minute until thickened.

6 Return the tofu to the wok with the green spring onions. Simmer gently for 1–2 minutes. Serve at once, garnished with basil leaves, on a bed of rice noodles.

NUTRITION NOTES	
Per portion:	
Energy	90kcals/374kJ
Protein	4.5g
Fat	7.9g
Saturated fat	1.1g
Carbohydrate	0.4g
Sugar	0.2g
Fibre (NSP)	0g
Calcium	287mg

Crispy Noodles with Mixed Vegetables

In this dish, rice vermicelli noodles are deep fried until crisp, then tossed into a colourful mixture of stir-fried vegetables.

INGREDIENTS

Serves 3–4

pure vegetable oil, for deep frying
115g/4oz dried vermicelli rice noodles
   or cellophane noodles, broken into
   7.5cm/3in lengths
115g/4oz yard-long beans or green
   beans, cut into short lengths
2.5cm/1in piece fresh root ginger, cut
   into shreds
1 fresh red chilli, sliced
115g/4oz/1½ cups fresh shiitake or
   button mushrooms, thickly sliced
2 large carrots, cut into fine sticks
2 courgettes, cut into fine sticks
a few Chinese cabbage leaves,
   coarsely shredded
75g/3oz/1 cup beansprouts
4 spring onions, cut into fine shreds
30ml/2 tbsp tamari
30ml/2 tbsp Chinese rice wine
5ml/1 tsp sugar
30ml/2 tbsp roughly torn
   coriander leaves

COOK'S TIPS

If a milder flavour is preferred, remove the seeds from the chilli.

Tamari is a type of soy sauce that is wheat free. It is available from Asian shops and some health food shops.

NUTRITION NOTES

Per portion:

Energy	245–184kcals/1021–766kJ
Protein	4.8–3.7g
Fat	8.16–6.1g
Saturated fat	1.2–0.9g
Carbohydrate	37–27.5g
Sugar	5.2–3.9g
Fibre (NSP)	2.9–2.2g
Calcium	54–41mg

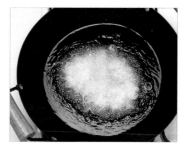

1 Half-fill a wok with oil and heat it to 180°C/350°F. Deep fry the raw noodles, a handful at a time, for 1–2 minutes until puffed and crispy. Drain on kitchen paper. Carefully pour off all but 30ml/2 tbsp of the oil.

2 Reheat the oil in the wok. When hot, add the beans and stir-fry for 2–3 minutes. Add the ginger, red chilli, mushrooms, carrots and courgettes and stir fry for 1–2 minutes.

3 Add the Chinese cabbage, beansprouts and spring onions to the wok. Stir-fry for 1 minute, then add the tamari, rice wine and sugar. Cook, stirring, for about 30 seconds.

4 Add the noodles and coriander and toss to mix, taking care not to crush the noodles too much. Serve at once, piled up on a plate.

FREE FROM

DESSERTS AND BAKES

You do not need to miss out on delicious desserts and bakes if you

are on a restricted diet. The fresh summer fruits in Iced Oranges or

Strawberries in Spiced Grape Jelly are impossible to resist.

Or try the mouthwatering Dutch Apple Cake; it will satisfy even the

sweetest tooth. Also in this selection are savoury Chive and Potato

Scones and Red Lentil Dosas, which make ideal snacks or

accompaniments to meat or vegetarian meals.

Pears with Ginger and Star Anise

FREE
FROM

Star anise and ginger give a refreshing twist to these poached pears. Serve them chilled.

INGREDIENTS

Serves 4
75g/3oz/6 tbsp caster sugar
300ml/ ½ pint/1¼ cups white
 dessert wine
thinly pared rind and juice of 1 lemon
7.5cm/3in piece fresh root
 ginger, bruised
5 star anise
10 cloves
600ml/1 pint/2½ cups cold water
6 slightly unripe pears
25g/1oz/3 tbsp drained, stem ginger
 in syrup, sliced
fromage frais, to serve (optional)

1 Place the caster sugar, dessert wine, lemon rind and juice, fresh root ginger, star anise, cloves and water into a saucepan just large enough to hold the pears snugly in an upright position. Bring to the boil.

2 Meanwhile, peel the pears, leaving the stems intact. Add them to the wine mixture, making sure that they are totally immersed in the liquid.

3 Return the wine mixture to the boil, lower the heat, cover and simmer for 15–20 minutes or until the pears are tender. Lift out the pears with a slotted spoon and place them in a heatproof dish.

4 Boil the wine syrup rapidly until it is reduced by about half, then pour over the pears. Allow them to cool, then chill.

5 Cut the pears into thick slices and arrange these on four serving plates. Remove the ginger and whole spices from the wine sauce, stir in the sliced stem ginger and spoon the sauce over the pears. Serve with fromage frais, if you like.

NUTRITION NOTES	
Per portion:	
Energy	190kcals/807kJ
Protein	0.8g
Fat	0.3g
Saturated fat	0g
Carbohydrate	45g
Sugar	44.7g
Fibre (NSP)	5.2g
Calcium	32mg

Spiced Figs with Honey and Orange

Fresh figs, cooked until tender in an orange-flavoured honey syrup that is scented with spices.

INGREDIENTS

Serves 6
450ml/¾ pint/1⅞ cups fresh
 orange juice
75g/3oz/⅓ cup clear honey
50g/2oz/¼ cup caster sugar
1 small orange
8 whole cloves
450g/1lb fresh figs
1 cinnamon stick
mint sprigs or bay leaves, to decorate

1 Put the orange juice, honey and sugar in a heavy-based saucepan and heat gently until the sugar has dissolved, stirring occasionally.

2 Stud the orange with the cloves and add to the syrup with the figs and cinnamon. Cover and simmer very gently for 5–10 minutes until the figs are softened. Transfer to a serving dish and leave to cool. Serve decorated with mint sprigs or bay leaves.

FREE
FROM

— NUTRITION NOTES —

Per portion:

Energy	60kcals/258kJ
Protein	1g
Fat	0.2g
Saturated fat	0g
Carbohydrate	10.3g
Sugar	10.3g
Fibre (NSP)	1.1g
Calcium	31mg

--- COOK'S TIP ---

Any variety of figs can be used in this recipe, their ripeness determining the cooking time. Choose ones that are plump and firm, and use quickly as they don't store well.

Iced Oranges

These pretty little sorbets served in the fruit shell were originally sold in the beach cafés in the south of France.

Ingredients

Serves 8
150g/5oz/⅔ cup granulated sugar
juice of 1 lemon
14 medium oranges
8 fresh bay leaves, to decorate

1 Put the sugar in a heavy-based pan. Add half the lemon juice, and 120ml/4fl oz/½ cup water. Cook over a low heat until the sugar has dissolved. Bring to the boil, and boil for 2–3 minutes, until the syrup is clear. Set aside and leave to cool.

2 Slice the tops off eight of the oranges, to make "hats". Scoop out the flesh of the oranges, and reserve in a bowl. Put the empty orange shells and "hats" on a tray and place in the freezer until needed.

3 Grate the rind of the remaining oranges and add to the syrup.

4 Squeeze the juice from the oranges, and from the reserved flesh. There should be 750ml/1¼ pints/3 cups of juice. If your oranges do not produce enough juice, squeeze another or top up with bought orange juice.

5 Stir the orange juice, the remaining lemon juice and 90ml/6 tbsp water into the syrup. Taste, adding more lemon juice or sugar, if you wish. Pour the mixture into a shallow freezer container and freeze for 3 hours.

6 Tip the mixture into a bowl, and whisk thoroughly to break down the ice crystals. Freeze for 4 hours more, until firm, but not solid.

7 Pack the mixture into the orange shells, mounding it up, and set the "hats" on top. Freeze until ready to serve. Just before serving, push a skewer into the tops of the "hats" to make a hole and push in a bay leaf.

— Nutrition Notes —	
Per portion:	
Energy	177kcals/757kJ
Protein	3g
Fat	0.2g
Saturated fat	0g
Carbohydrate	43.3g
Sugar	43.3g
Fibre (NSP)	4.7g
Calcium	133mg

Blackcurrant Sorbet

This luscious sorbet is easily made by hand, but it is important to alternately freeze and blend or process the mixture five or six times to get the best result. If you make lots of ice cream and sorbets, it is worth investing in an electric ice cream maker.

INGREDIENTS

Serves 6

115g/4oz/½ cup caster sugar
225g/8oz/2 cups fresh or frozen
   blackcurrants
5ml/1 tsp lemon juice
30ml/2 tbsp crème de cassis or other
   blackcurrant liqueur (optional)
2 egg whites (optional)

1 Pour 300ml/½ pint/1¼ cups water into a saucepan and add the sugar. Place over a low heat until the sugar has dissolved. Bring to the boil and boil rapidly for 10 minutes, then set the syrup aside to cool.

2 Meanwhile, cook the blackcurrants in a saucepan with 30ml/2 tbsp water over a low heat for 5–7 minutes until tender.

3 Press the cooked blackcurrants and their juice through a sieve placed over a jug. Stir the resulting blackcurrant purée into the syrup with the lemon juice and the blackcurrant liqueur, if using. Allow to cool completely, then chill for 1 hour.

4 Pour the chilled blackcurrant syrup into a freezerproof bowl; freeze until slushy, removing and whisking occasionally until it reaches this point. Whisk the egg whites, if using, in a grease-free bowl until they form soft peaks, then gently fold into the semi-frozen blackcurrant mixture.

5 Freeze the mixture again until firm, then spoon into a food processor or blender and process. Alternately freeze and process or blend until completely smooth. Serve the sorbet straight from the freezer.

NUTRITION NOTES	
Per portion:	
Energy	103kcals/438kJ
Protein	1.3g
Fat	0g
Saturated fat	0g
Carbohydrate	24.2g
Sugar	24.2g
Fibre (NSP)	1.3g
Calcium	25mg

FREE FROM

Strawberries in Spiced Grape Jelly

What better way to celebrate the strawberry season than with this summer dessert. Raspberries make the perfect alternative if you are allergic to strawberries.

INGREDIENTS

Serves 4
450ml/ ¾ pint/1⅞ cups red grape juice
1 cinnamon stick
1 small orange
15ml/1 tbsp/1 sachet powdered gelatine
225g/8oz strawberries, chopped
strawberries and shreds of orange rind, to decorate

1 Place the grape juice in a pan with the cinnamon. Thinly pare the rind from the orange and add to the pan. Infuse over a very low heat for 10 minutes, then remove the cinnamon and orange rind.

2 Squeeze the juice from the orange and sprinkle the gelatine over the top. Leave to swell, then stir into the grape juice to dissolve. Allow to cool until just beginning to set.

3 Stir the strawberries into the setting jelly and quickly tip into a l litre/ 1¾ pint/4 cup mould or serving dish. Chill until set.

4 To turn out, dip the mould quickly into hot water and invert on to a serving plate. Decorate with fresh strawberries and shreds of orange rind.

NUTRITION NOTES	
Per portion:	
Energy	85kcals/347kJ
Protein	1.2g
Fat	0.2g
Saturated fat	0g
Carbohydrate	19.9g
Sugar	19.9g
Fibre (NSP)	1g
Calcium	49mg

Portuguese Rice Pudding

This recipe uses egg yolks that are only very lightly cooked, omit them, if you wish, and use soya milk in place of cow's milk.

INGREDIENTS

Serves 4–6
175g/6oz pudding rice
600ml/1 pint/2½ cups creamy milk
65g/2½oz/5 tbsp butter or pure
   vegetable margarine
2–3 strips pared lemon rind
115g/4oz/½ cup caster sugar
4 egg yolks (optional)
salt
ground cinnamon, for sprinkling

1 Cook the rice in plenty of lightly salted water for about 5 minutes so that it is still uncooked but has lost its brittleness.

2 Drain well and then place in a saucepan with the milk, butter or margarine and lemon rind. Very slowly bring to the boil, then cover and simmer over a low heat for about 20 minutes until the rice is thick and creamy.

3 Turn off the heat and allow the rice mixture to cool a little. Remove and discard the lemon rind and then stir in the sugar and egg yolks, if using.

4 Divide among 4–6 serving bowls and dust with ground cinnamon. Cool and serve.

— NUTRITION NOTES —	
Per portion:	
Energy	568–378kcals/2375–1583kJ
Protein	12.1–8g
Fat	27–18g
Saturated fat	15.4–10.2g
Carbohydrate	70–47g
Sugar	37–24g
Fibre (NSP)	0g
Calcium	230–154mg

Dutch Apple Cake

The apple topping makes this gluten-free cake really moist and a real treat for those following a special diet.

INGREDIENTS

Makes 8–10 slices
250g/9oz/2¼ cups gluten-free
  self-raising flour
5ml/1 tsp ground cinnamon
130g/4½oz/generous ½ cup
  caster sugar
50g/2oz/4tbs pure vegetable
  margarine, melted
2 large eggs, beaten
150ml/¼ pint/⅔ cup soya milk

For the topping
2 Cox's Orange Pippin apples
15ml/1 tbsp pure vegetable
  margarine, melted
30ml/2 tbsp demerara sugar
1.5ml/¼ tsp ground cinnamon

1 Preheat the oven to 200°C/400°F/ Gas 6. Grease and line a 20cm/8in round cake tin. Sift the flour and cinnamon into a mixing bowl. Stir in the caster sugar. In a separate bowl, whisk the melted margarine, eggs and milk, then stir into the dry ingredients.

2 Pour into the prepared tin, smooth the surface, then make a shallow hollow around the edge of the mixture.

NUTRITION NOTES

Per portion:	
Energy	220kcals/932kJ
Protein	4.3g
Fat	5.6g
Saturated fat	1.6g
Carbohydrate	4.1g
Sugar	2.3g
Fibre (NSP)	0.1g
Calcium	110mg

3 Make the topping. Peel and core the apples, and slice into thin wedges. Arrange the slices around the hollow of the cake mixture. Brush with melted margarine, then scatter the demerara sugar and ground cinnamon over the top.

4 Bake for 45–50 minutes or until well risen and golden and a skewer inserted into the centre comes out clean. Remove from the tin, peel off the lining paper and serve hot, or cool on a wire rack before slicing.

Pear and Polenta Cake

INGREDIENTS

Makes 10 slices
175g/6oz/¾ cup golden caster sugar
4 ripe pears
juice of ½ lemon
30ml/2 tbsp clear honey
3 eggs
5ml/1 tsp pure vanilla essence
120ml/4fl oz/½ cup sunflower oil
115g/4oz/1 cup gluten-free
  self-raising flour
5ml/1 tsp gluten-free baking powder
50g/2oz/⅓ cup polenta

1 Preheat the oven to 180°C/350°F/ Gas 4. Grease and line a 21cm/ 8½in round cake tin. Scatter 30ml/ 2 tbsp of the caster sugar over the base of the prepared tin.

2 Peel, core and slice the pears and toss them in the lemon juice. Arrange on the base of the cake tin. Drizzle the honey over and set aside.

3 Mix together the eggs, vanilla essence and the remaining sugar in a bowl. Beat until thick and creamy, then gradually beat in the oil. Sift together the flour, baking powder and polenta and fold into the egg mixture.

4 Pour the mixture carefully over the pears. Bake for about 50 minutes or until a skewer inserted into the centre comes out clean. Cool in the tin for 10 minutes, then turn the cake out on to a plate and peel off the lining paper. Turn the cake over and serve.

NUTRITION NOTES

Per portion:	
Energy	241kcals/1014kJ
Protein	2.5g
Fat	9.1g
Saturated fat	1.1g
Carbohydrate	39.3g
Sugar	27.2g
Fibre (NSP)	1.75g
Calcium	50.5mg

Oatcakes

These oatcakes are delicious served as a snack with grapes and wedges of cheese. They are also good topped with thick honey for breakfast.

INGREDIENTS

Makes 8

175g/6oz/1 cup medium oatmeal, plus extra for sprinkling
2.5ml/½ tsp salt
pinch of bicarbonate of soda
15ml/1 tbsp pure vegetable margarine
75ml/5 tbsp water

COOK'S TIP

To achieve a neat round, place a 25cm/10in plate on top of the oatcake dough. Cut away any excess dough with a palette knife, then remove the plate.

1 Preheat the oven to 150°C/300°F/ Gas 2. Mix the oatmeal with the salt and bicarbonate of soda in a large mixing bowl.

2 Melt the margarine with the water in a small saucepan. Bring to the boil, then add to the oatmeal mixture and mix to a moist dough.

3 Turn the dough on to a surface sprinkled with extra oatmeal and knead to a smooth ball. Turn a large baking sheet upside-down, grease it, sprinkle it lightly with oatmeal and place the ball of dough on top. Sprinkle the dough with oatmeal, then roll out to a 25cm/10in round.

4 Cut the round into eight sections, ease them apart slightly and bake for about 50–60 minutes until crisp.

5 Leave to cool on the baking sheet, then carefully remove the oatcakes with a palette knife.

NUTRITION NOTES

Per portion:
Energy	101kcals/428kJ
Protein	2.7g
Fat	3.4g
Saturated fat	0.7g
Carbohydrate	15.9g
Sugar	0g
Fibre (NSP)	1.5g
Calcium	12mg

Chive and Potato Scones

These little scones make an ideal breakfast treat for those following a wheat- or gluten-free diet.

INGREDIENTS

Makes 20

450g/1lb potatoes, peeled and cut into chunks
115g/4oz/1 cup plain gluten-free flour, sifted
45ml/3 tbsp olive oil
30ml/2 tbsp snipped chives
vegetable oil, for greasing
salt and ground black pepper
grilled bacon and tomatoes, to serve

VARIATION

If you are not following a gluten- or wheat-free diet, use plain flour, if you wish.

FREE FROM

1 Cook the potatoes in a saucepan of boiling salted water for 15 minutes or until tender, then drain thoroughly. Return the potatoes to the clean pan and mash them.

NUTRITION NOTES

Per portion:

Energy	50kcals/215kJ
Protein	1.1g
Fat	1.7g
Saturated fat	0.2g
Carbohydrate	8.3g
Sugar	0.4g
Fibre (NSP)	0.5g
Calcium	9.2mg

2 Add the flour, olive oil and snipped chives with a little salt and pepper to the hot mashed potato in the pan. Mix to a soft dough.

3 Roll out the dough on a surface dusted with gluten-free flour to a thickness of 5mm/¼ in; cut out rounds with a 5cm/2in pastry cutter.

4 Lightly grease, then heat a griddle or frying pan. Place the potato rounds on the hot griddle or frying pan. Cook over a low heat, in batches if necessary, for about 10 minutes, turning once, until the scones are golden brown on both sides. Serve hot with grilled bacon slices and tomatoes.

Red Lentil Dosas

Dosas are southern Indian breads. They are very different from traditional north Indian breads, such as chapatis, as they are made from lentils and rice rather than flour, so they are the perfect choice for people who have a gluten or wheat allergy. *Dosas* are like pancakes and are delicious freshly cooked for breakfast, or as an accompaniment to main meals, especially stews, curries and rice dishes.

INGREDIENTS

Makes 6 dosas
150g/5oz/¾ cup long grain rice
50g/2oz/¼ cup red lentils
5ml/1 tsp salt
2.5ml/½ tsp ground turmeric
2.5ml/½ tsp ground black pepper
30ml/2 tbsp chopped fresh coriander
oil, for frying and drizzling

VARIATION

To make spicy coconut *dosas*, add 60ml/ 4 tbsp grated coconut, 15ml/1 tbsp grated fresh root ginger and 1 finely chopped chilli to the batter just before cooking.

NUTRITION NOTES

Per portion:	
Energy	138kcals/588kJ
Protein	3.8g
Fat	2.8g
Saturated fat	0.5g
Carbohydrate	26.1g
Sugar	0.2g
Fibre (NSP)	0.5g
Calcium	17mg

1 Place the rice and lentils in a bowl, cover with 250ml/8fl oz/1 cup warm water and leave to soak for 8 hours, then drain off the water and reserve. Place the rice and lentils in a food processor and blend until smooth. Blend in the reserved water.

2 Transfer to a bowl, cover with clear film and leave in a warm place to ferment for about 24 hours.

3 Stir in the salt, turmeric, pepper and coriander. Heat a heavy-based frying pan over a medium heat for a few minutes until hot. Smear with a little oil and add about 30–45ml/ 2–3 tbsp of the batter.

4 Using the rounded bottom of a soup spoon, gently spread the batter out, using a circular motion, to make a 15cm/6in diameter *dosa*.

5 Cook for 1½–2 minutes, or until set. Drizzle a little oil over the *dosa* and around the edges. Turn over and cook for about 1 minute, or until golden. Keep warm in a low oven or over simmering water while cooking the remaining *dosas*. Serve warm.

INFORMATION FILE

USEFUL ADDRESSES

**Allergy and Environmental
Sensitivity Support and Research
Association (Australia)**
PO Box 298
Ringwood
Victoria 3134
Australia
Tel: (61) 39888 1282

The Anaphylaxis Campaign
PO Box 149
Fleet, Hampshire GU13 9XU
Tel: 01252 542029

The Brain Foundation (Australia)
PO Box 579
Suite 21, Regent House
Alexander Street
Crow's Nest, Sydney, NSW 2065
Tel: (61) 29437 5967

The British Allergy Foundation
Deepdene House
30 Bellegrove Road
Welling
Kent DA16 3PY
Tel: 0181 303 8525/8583
(Helpline: 0891 516500)

**The National Society for Research
into Allergy**
P.O. Box 45
Hinkley
Leicestershire LE10 1JY
Tel: 01455 851546

The British Nutrition Foundation
High Holborn House
52-54 High Holborn
London WC1V 6RQ
Tel: 0171 404 6504

Canadian Coeliac Association
6519B Mississauga Road
Ontario L5N 1A6
Tel: (1) 905 567 7195

The Coeliac Society of Australia
PO Box 271
Wahroonga 2076 NSW
Tel: (61) 29411 4100

**The Coeliac Society of Great
Britain**
PO Box 220
High Wycombe, Bucks. HP11 2HY
Tel: 01494 437278

**The Coeliac Society of South
Africa**
Box No 64203
Highland North 2073, Johannesburg
Tel: (27) 11 440 3431

**The Hyperactive Children's
Support Group**
71 Whyke Lane
Chichester, Sussex PO19 2LD
Tel: 01903 725182

**Hyperactivity Association
(NSW Australia)**
15/29 Bertram Street
Chatswood 2067 NSW
Tel: (61) 29411 2186

Medic Alert
(Emergency identification system)
1 Bridge Wharf
156 Caledonian Road
London N1 9UU
Tel: 0800 581420

The Migraine Trust
45 Great Ormond Street
London WC1N 3HZ
Tel: 0171 831 4818

**Ministry of Agriculture, Fisheries
and Food**
Joint Food Safety and Standards Group
Room 306 C
Ergon House, c/o Nobel House
17 Smith Square
London SW1P 3JR
Consumer Helpline: 0345 573012

**The National Asthma Campaign
(and Junior Asthma Club)**
Providence House
Providence Place
London N1 0NT
Tel: 0171 226 2260
(Helpline: 0345 010203)

**The National Dairy Council
Nutrition Service**
5–7 John Princes Street
London W1M 0AP
Tel: 0171 499 7822

The National Eczema Society
163 Eversholt Street
London NW1 1BU
Tel: 0171 388 4097

MAIL ORDER FOODS

Allergycare
(Specialist foods)
1 Church Square
Taunton, Somerset TA1 1SA
Tel: 01823 325022/3

Doves Farm Foods Ltd
(Specialist flours)
Salisbury Road
Hungerford
Berks. RG17 0RF
Tel: 01488 684880

Trufree Foods
(Mail order gluten- and wheat-free
flours)
225 Putney Bridge Road
London SW15 2PY
Tel: 0181 874 1130

FURTHER READING
*The Complete Guide to Food Allergy
and Intolerance*
by Professor Jonathan Brostoff and
Linda Gamlin – Bloomsbury

INDEX